J. WESTON WALCH PUBLISHER
Portland, Maine

Content Writing Strategies

Language Arts

Anna Montuori

User's Guide
to
Walch Reproducible Books

Purchasers of this book are granted the right to reproduce all pages where this symbol appears.

This permission is limited to a single teacher, for classroom use only.

Any questions regarding this policy or requests to purchase further reproduction rights should be addressed to:

> Permissions Editor
> J. Weston Walch, Publisher
> 321 Valley Street • P.O. Box 658
> Portland, Maine 04104-0658

1 2 3 4 5 6 7 8 9 10

ISBN 0-8251-4329-2

Copyright © 2002
J. Weston Walch, Publisher
P. O. Box 658 • Portland, Maine 04104-0658
www.walch.com

Printed in the United States of America

Contents

Introduction v

Part 1: Prewriting 1
   Lesson 1: Writing Process Review 2
   Lesson 2: Brainstorming 3
   Lesson 3: Narrowing Your Topic 5
   Lesson 4: Purpose 6
   Lesson 5: Audience 7

Part 2: Writing Strategies 9
   Lesson 6: Drafting 10
   Lesson 7: Main Idea and Details 11
   Lesson 8: Opinion and Supporting Evidence 22
   Lesson 9: Compare and Contrast 32
   Lesson 10: Cause and Effect 43
   Lesson 11: Chronological Order 53

Part 3: Practice Readings 63
   Practice Reading A: Female Athletes and Injury 64
   Practice Reading B: It Can Only Be Love 66
   Practice Reading C: Sandra Cisneros: Author 69
   Practice Reading D: Antonia Hernandez: Civil Rights Lawyer 71

Part 4: Graphic Organizers 73
   Brainstorming Web 74
   Main Idea and Details Chart 75
   Opinion and Supporting Evidence Chart 76
   Compare and Contrast (Venn) Diagram 77
   Cause and Effect Chart 78
   Chronological Order Chart 79
   Revising Checklist 80
   Proofreading Checklist 81
   Peer-Editing Form 82

Part 5: Teacher's Guide 83
   Teaching Tips and Answer Key 84
   Assessment Rubric 87

INTRODUCTION

The *Content-Area Writing Strategies* books teach students to write essays for classroom assignments. The writing process is reviewed, and models show good writing in action.

Students move from reading about writing, through observing good writing, to creating their own solid written pieces. They learn to recognize common language arts writing patterns and employ them themselves to write effective essays. These patterns are main idea and details, opinion and supporting evidence, compare and contrast, cause and effect, and chronological order.

Graphic organizers help students generate and clarify their thoughts during the prewriting and writing stages of the writing process. These graphic organizers are embedded in the instructional pages; blanks are also found in Part 4 of this book. A revising checklist and a peer-editing form aid in the revision stage, and a proofreading checklist reminds students of the mechanics of strong writing. A grading rubric simplifies the teacher's task of scoring!

Classroom Management

Content-Area Writing Strategies is easy to use. Each lesson is a self-contained study of a part of the writing process. Simply photocopy the lesson and distribute it. You may want to model some of the Try It sections on the board or on a transparency if students need a little more help identifying the elements being discussed in a particular lesson. Lessons build on earlier lessons, so it is suggested that the lessons be explored in order.

Part 1: Prewriting

Part 1 of this book concentrates on prewriting, guiding students through the steps that lead up to writing: brainstorming, narrowing a topic, clarifying purpose, and identifying audience. This section emphasizes the importance (necessity!) of planning in creating a worthwhile and successful final product.

Part 2: Writing Strategies

This section deals with writing strategies, giving students abundant opportunities to see good writing, and then to try it themselves. It also offers useful graphic organizers to help students generate a blueprint of their piece before it is written. This helps students clarify and organize their ideas, and keeps them on track while they are writing.

Part 3: Practice Readings

Part 3 of *Content-Area Writing Strategies* provides longer practice readings. You may wish to assign one of the suggested essay questions listed in the Teaching Tips section at the end of this book, have students choose a question from the list, or encourage students to generate their own thesis statements based on the reading.

Part 4: Graphic Organizers

This section contains blank graphic organizers for use with any writing assignment. A revising checklist, peer-editing form, and a proofreading checklist are also included in this section.

Part 5: Teacher's Guide

The Teaching Tips and Answer Key provide ideas for each lesson, with answers for those exercises requiring them. This is also where you will find suggestions for essay questions for the practice readings (found in Part 3 of the instruction). The assessment rubric simplifies the task of scoring. You may want to customize the rubric by adding categories to the "Other" section, by adjusting point values, or by modifying the "Criteria."

The reading-writing connection is a strong one; practicing and strengthening one improves the other. *Content-Area Reading Strategies* is a companion series to this one, focusing on reading comprehension in the disciplines of language arts, social studies, science, and mathematics. The *Content-Area Vocabulary Strategies* series concentrates on using context clues and other strategies to decipher unfamiliar vocabulary in content-area reading.

PART 1
Prewriting

Lesson 1
Writing Process Review

The Writing Process

When you read a published piece of writing, you expect it to be neat, to be free of errors, to make a point, and to follow some logical order. If the piece does not meet these expectations, your reading experience will be unsatisfactory—if you bother to finish reading at all.

A good written piece does not flow from a pen or spew from a printer in its finished form. Writing is a process. This process has four stages: prewriting, drafting, revising, and publishing.

Parts of an Essay

When you follow the writing process, your goal is to produce a solid essay. Your essay will contain an introduction, a body, and a conclusion.

The **introduction** is the beginning of your essay. This is where your thesis statement or topic sentence appears. Your thesis statement tells the reader what the essay will prove or show or discuss.

The **body** supplies the support for your thesis statement. It follows through on what the introduction has promised. In general, an essay will have at least three body paragraphs that show the truth of the thesis statement.

The **conclusion** restates the thesis statement or topic sentence and brings the essay to a logical and satisfying close.

Prewriting

Prewriting, as its name suggests, is something you do *before* you write an essay or other written work. Prewriting involves thinking and planning. During prewriting, you decide what and how you will write.

This stage of the writing process contains several steps, which you will learn about in the lessons that follow.

- brainstorming ideas
- narrowing your topic
- defining your purpose for writing
- identifying your audience

Lesson 2
Brainstorming

Brainstorming Brainstorming allows you to explore the ins and outs of a topic. It generates ideas you can build on. It gives you a way to uncover what you already know about a topic. And it can be fun!

During brainstorming, let your thoughts run wild. Don't place restrictions on your thinking. Just jot down what comes into your mind.

Brainstorming Web To practice brainstorming, imagine that you have to respond to the following essay question: *Discuss zoos in modern society.*

To begin a brainstorming session, turn the essay question into a category heading. In this case, you might write *zoos today* in the center of your web.

Then jump-start your thinking by asking yourself questions about the topic. *What are zoos? What can be seen at zoos? Why do people visit zoos? Are some exhibits more popular than others?*

Note your responses on your web, writing your ideas in circles. Show connections between ideas with lines. Before you know it, your brainstorming web might look something like this.

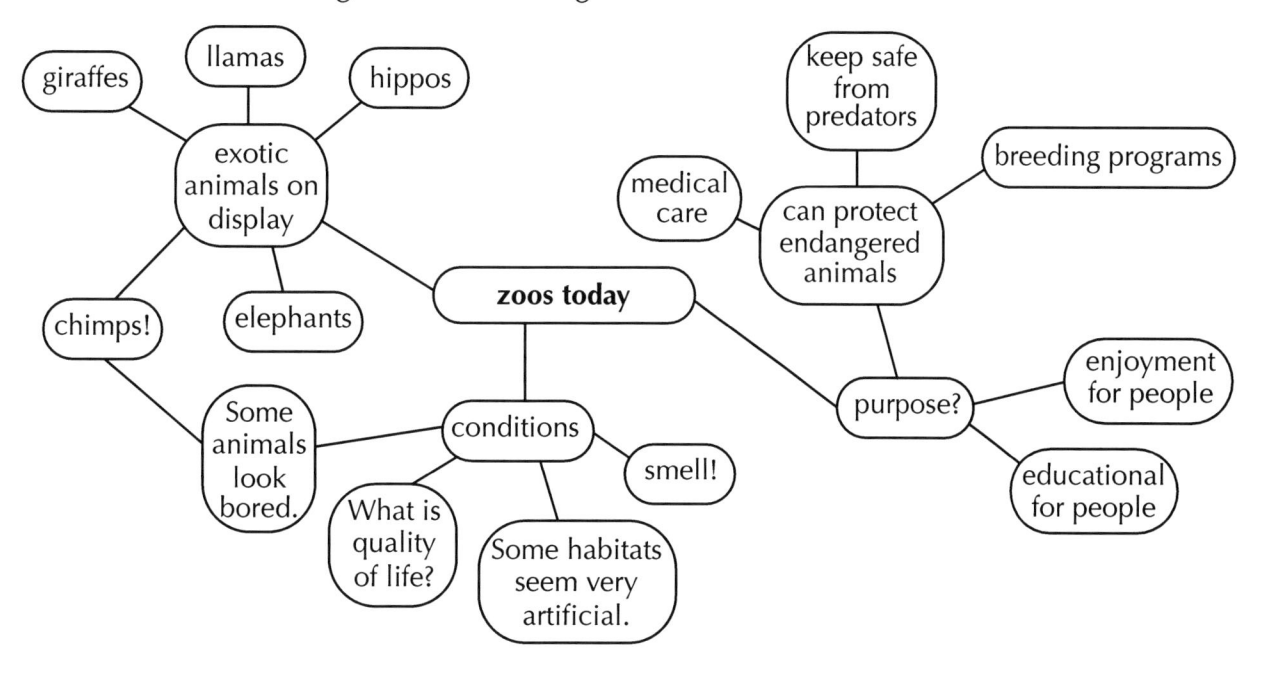

© 2002 J. Weston Walch, Publisher — Content-Area Writing Strategies: Language Arts

Brainstorming *(continued)*

Try It Now practice brainstorming. Imagine that you have been assigned to write an essay on the broad topic of "sharks." Brainstorm what you know about, think of, and associate with sharks. Remember not to censor yourself. Ask yourself questions and write your answers. Show how ideas are connected by linking them with lines. Use the web below as a base. Add or remove circles and lines as needed.

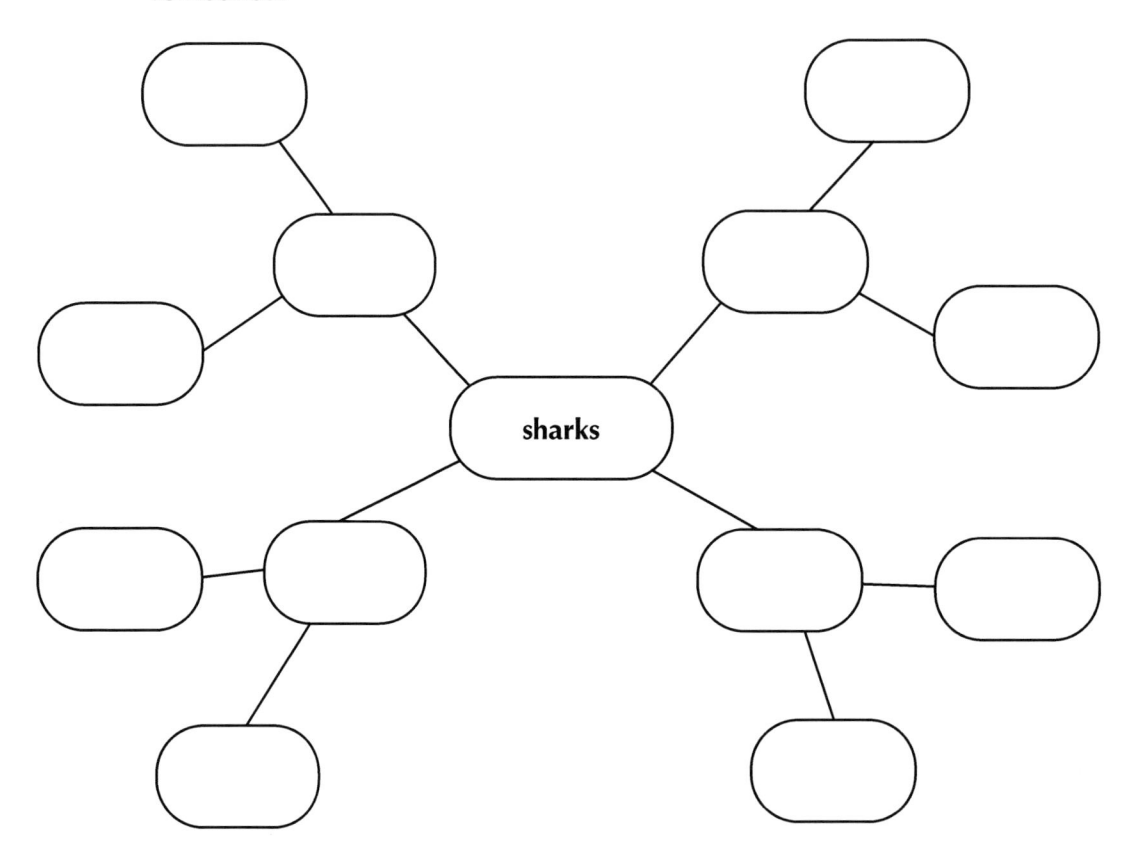

© 2002 J. Weston Walch, Publisher

Content-Area Writing Strategies: Language Arts

LESSON 3
Narrowing Your Topic

From Broad to Narrow

After your thoughts about a topic have been exhausted, it is time to step back from your brainstorming web and analyze it. Your goal is to recognize patterns that will help you decide on a narrower, more manageable topic to write about in an essay.

Analyze the Web

Review the sample brainstorming web about zoos on page 3. Do you see any patterns? Are there some areas that are more filled-in than others? Do the words or punctuation show that the author feels strongly about a certain aspect of the topic? Does the author know a lot about one area? Questions like these uncover interest, knowledge, and strong feelings that may make a particular part of a topic satisfying to write about.

Imagine that you filled in the web about zoos and are ready to analyze it. Your conversation with yourself might go something like this:

> I identified some of the attractions of zoos—I listed mostly exotic animals that do not normally live in this part of the world. I noted reasons for zoos—I guess that in certain cases, zoos help animals, like if they are endangered. But I think that zoos seem to exist mainly to entertain people. I'm not sure that is a good enough reason to keep zoos—especially since I listed negative effects on animals. Who really benefits from zoos? The people who own them. Animals have no use for the money they bring in. Some animals look sad, and I read that many animals don't live very long in captivity. I don't like zoos at all! I think they should be banned, except to save endangered species. People can look at exotic animals on television; they don't need to have animals locked up for that.

This analysis has led to a narrowed topic: reasons that zoos should be banned. This topic is manageable, and the author already has some background information. The author can now focus the essay, make a reasoned point, and keep the essay to a readable length.

Try It

Now look at the web you filled out for your hypothetical essay on sharks. Analyze your web by looking for patterns that show where your interest and knowledge lie. Think about your web. Then write a possible narrowed topic.

_____

LESSON 4
Purpose

Why Are You Writing *This* Essay?

Of course, you probably write most essays because they have been assigned. Beyond that, however, is a **purpose** specific to your essay—why you wrote what you wrote.

Generally, all authors have one purpose in mind when they write: to persuade readers of the validity of the written ideas. This broad purpose can be broken down into many, more specific, purposes. Journalists write to provide factual information about controversial issues. Writers of editorials want to convince readers of an opinion. Historians write to record the past. Scientists explain experiments or phenomena. Reviewers evaluate a book or a performance. An author's purpose is the goal he or she wishes to achieve through writing.

Often your teacher—or a printed question on a test—will state the general purpose of an assigned essay. During the first week of school, for example, you might be asked to describe your summer vacation. Your language arts teacher might ask you to discuss a major theme of a novel, or to compare and contrast two characters from the book. A test question might ask you to write about the events that led up to the American Revolution. It will still be up to you to put that general purpose into your own words, and to fulfill it.

State Your Purpose

Whatever the particular assignment and topic are, you will have to state your purpose—what you plan to show—early on in your essay. This statement of purpose is often called a *thesis statement* or a *topic sentence*. Your thesis statement is one sentence that takes a stance about your narrowed topic.

To see how to transform a narrowed topic into a thesis statement, think back to the zoo web. The ideas in the web showed an interest in a narrow topic: the negative aspects of zoos. The author analyzed the ideas and clarified what she wanted to show in an essay: Zoos should be banned because they are not in the animals' best interest. Voilà! A thesis statement is born.

Try It

Now it's time to try writing a thesis statement for your imaginary essay on sharks. Think about your narrowed topic, and take a position about it. Write that position in one sentence that sums up what you will show in your essay on sharks.

Lesson 5
Audience

Who Will Read This Essay?

Any communication is intended for an **audience**. A memo from a supervisor may be intended for that person's boss, or for an employee. A receipt in a store will be read by a customer—and a cashier if the item is returned. An instruction manual is written to help the new owner use the product.

What does it matter who will read what you write? Well, if you were the owner of a new computer, you would be upset if the instructions you got were about advanced programming, when what you were looking for was how to plug in the machine!

Who the audience for your essay is affects how and what you write. If your audience is your teacher and maybe your classmates, and the topic is something you have been discussing in class, you would probably assume that your readers would understand the concepts and vocabulary you would normally use. If, however, your audience was a younger class, you might use less specialized vocabulary and shorter sentences. If you were writing a letter to the editor about a subject that was not common knowledge, you would have to explain the concept so people could understand your letter. You must consider your audience for your writing to be effective.

Good Writing Tip: Use Standard English

When you are writing formally, that is, in any situation other than a personal note, you should use Standard English. This means you should avoid slang expressions, incorrect grammar, and inappropriate words, even if all of these are part of the language you use with friends or at home.

Think about the essay on zoos. Since the audience for this essay is the classroom teacher and classmates, the language would be Standard English. Since the audience has the same level of knowledge and experience as the author, the vocabulary would be straightforward—the readers are neither zoologists nor people who have never heard of zoos. Since the essay is about an opinion, not a legal argument, for example, the ideas will be relatively simple rather than complex.

Audience *(continued)*

Considering Your Audience

1. Now consider the essay about sharks. How would you write your essay if your audience were a panel of marine biologists?

2. How would you adjust your writing if your audience were a kindergarten class?

3. How would you write if this were not an essay for school but a feature article in the local newspaper?

Part 2
Writing Strategies

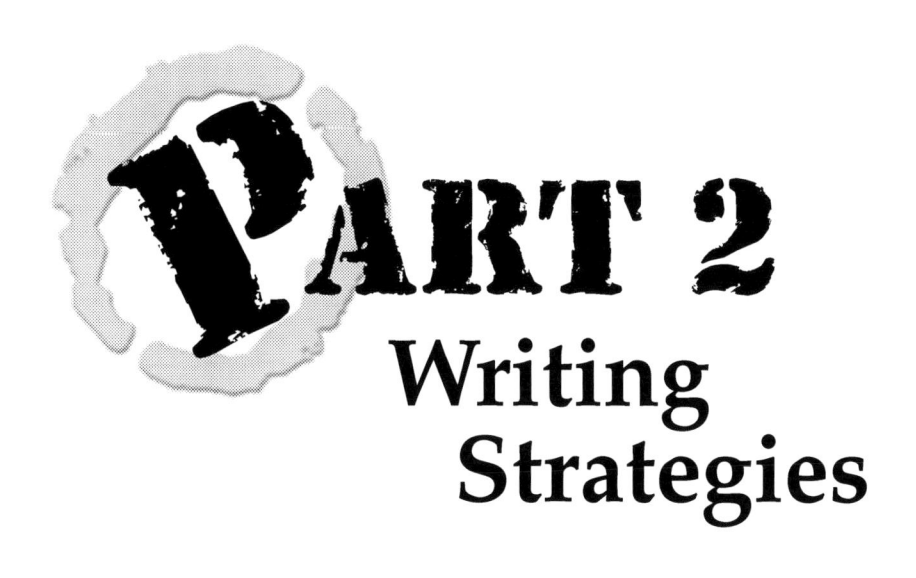

Lesson 6
Drafting

The First Draft

Once you have done the prewriting steps, you are ready to begin **drafting**, or writing. Some people think that drafting is an extension of brainstorming. This is not so! When you sit down to draft an essay, your goal is a well-organized and clear piece of writing. You will write several drafts to reach essay perfection, but you should put your best effort into each one. The writing done in the prewriting steps is more like jotting, or noting. When you draft, try to write in logical, complete sentences.

In general, an essay should have at least five paragraphs: an introductory paragraph, at least three body paragraphs, and a concluding paragraph. A well-constructed paragraph is like a mini version of an essay: It should have a topic sentence, supporting sentences, and a concluding sentence.

Common Patterns in Language Arts

Of course, all writing can be considered language arts writing, because it involves language. But there are some common patterns that you are likely to use when writing for language arts classes. Each of these patterns will be shown and practiced in the lessons ahead.

- Main ideas and details
- Opinion and supporting evidence
- Compare and contrast
- Cause and effect
- Chronological order

1. Think about the types of writing you do daily. List some of them here.

2. What types of writing do you do specifically for language arts?

© 2002 J. Weston Walch, Publisher

Lesson 7
Main Idea and Details

One of the most common writing patterns you will see is organized according to main idea and details. In this pattern, the main idea is presented in the first paragraph. Then details that support or prove that idea follow in the body paragraphs. The final, or concluding, paragraph restates the main idea and refers to the details.

Model

Read the following paragraph about the ocean. See if you can find the main idea and details.

> The bottom of the ocean is the most mysterious place on Earth. Every so often, parts of a deep-sea animal, such as an eight-foot-long tentacle or a section of a giant worm, wash up on shore. Even the most knowledgeable marine biologists have to scratch their heads and wonder, "What is that thing?" Despite the physical evidence pointing to the existence of such creatures as the giant squid, razor-fanged viperfish, and other animals, no one truly knows what lurks in the coldest, darkest depths of the ocean. This great mystery is due in large part to deep-sea pressure, an intense, crushing force that increases with depth. Humans experience a less intense form of this pressure when they dive into the deep end of a swimming pool, for example. Deep-sea pressure makes it impossible for humans to travel to the ocean floor to observe deep-sea life forms. Similarly, deep-sea life forms cannot be brought to the surface without being destroyed by the drastic pressure change. Until humans discover a way to explore the great depths of the oceans, what lives in its farthest reaches will remain a mystery.

The main idea of this paragraph is found in the first sentence: "The bottom of the ocean is the most mysterious place on Earth." Did you find the supporting details that illustrate the main idea? The first one follows soon after the main idea: "Even the most knowledgeable marine biologists have to scratch their heads and wonder, 'What is that thing?'" This sentence shows that the ocean bottom is indeed mysterious, even to experts. The next detail explains one reason for the mystery: "This great mystery is due in large part to deep-sea pressure, an intense, crushing force that increases with depth." The next details explain the consequences of pressure: "Deep-sea pressure makes it impossible for humans to travel to the ocean floor to observe deep-sea life forms. Similarly, deep-sea life forms cannot be brought to the surface without

Main Idea and Details *(continued)*

being destroyed by the drastic pressure change." The very last sentence is the conclusion: "Until humans discover a way to explore the great depths of the oceans, what lives in its farthest reaches will remain a mystery." The concluding sentence restates the main idea—that the bottom of the ocean is a mystery—and incorporates the details—that deep-sea pressure has so far kept humans from knowing about the ocean floor.

Try It

Read the following passage carefully, keeping in mind that this selection features a main-idea-and-details pattern. When you have finished reading, look at the list that follows. See if you can tell the main ideas from the details.

> Even though the saying "the only constant in life is change" is proven true each and every day, humans still have great difficulty accepting the unexpected. Maxwell, a single father of two, discovered how unprepared he was to deal with the unexpected. He spent thirty-six hours laundering, folding, and packing clothes for his two children and himself so that they could catch a 9 A.M. flight to Disney World. At the airport, Maxwell was told that there had been a mistake made with his reservations and that one of his tickets was for a flight that had already left for Florida. Maxwell couldn't send his kids ahead to Florida without him, nor could he leave one of his kids behind to take a later flight, for they were only five and eight years old. Frustrated and angry, Maxwell canceled the trip altogether and returned home—to spend what was supposed to be a sun-and-fun-filled week watching videos at his condominium.
>
> Similarly, Corey learned a lot about his reaction to change when he took two days off from work to prepare for his wife Elle's arrival home from a three-week out-of-state training session. He cleaned their entire apartment from top to bottom; he ordered several bouquets of brightly colored flowers, which he placed strategically throughout their home; he cooked late into the evening, preparing his wife's all-time favorite foods. Just as he was lighting the candles for the romantic welcome-home dinner that he had prepared, the phone rang. It was Elle. Her flight had been delayed due to high winds and fog, and she had no idea when she would be arriving home. Obviously disappointed, Corey began to argue with her over the phone, demanding to know when she would be home.
>
> All in all, Maxwell and Corey's responses to the changes that were imposed on their plans only made their situations worse. Both should have taken a deep breath and realized that nothing in life is written in stone, and everything, even the best-laid plans, is subject to change.

Main Idea and Details *(continued)*

Did you find the main ideas and details? Write **MI** before main ideas and **D** before details.

1. _____ The saying "the only constant in life is change" is proven true each and every day.

2. _____ Humans have great difficulty accepting the unexpected.

3. _____ Maxwell discovered how unprepared he was to deal with the unexpected.

4. _____ Maxwell was told that there had been a mistake made with his reservations.

5. _____ Maxwell canceled the trip.

6. _____ Corey learned a lot about his reaction to change.

7. _____ Corey cleaned and cooked in preparation for his wife Elle's return home.

8. _____ Elle's flight had been delayed.

9. _____ Corey began to argue with Elle over the phone.

10. _____ Nothing in life is written in stone, and everything is subject to change.

Good Writing Tip: Write a Clear Thesis Statement

The key to writing a successful main-idea-and-details essay is organization. You want to clearly identify the main idea of the essay early on. To do this, you need to provide readers with a sentence that states what the main idea of the essay is. This sentence will become the thesis statement or controlling idea for the whole essay. Everything that you write must connect with the thesis statement.

Main Idea and Details *(continued)*

Good Writing Tip: Use Transitions

Transition words and phrases enhance an essay's organization. Transitions link thoughts together. Transitions may appear at the beginning of body paragraphs to link the thoughts in one paragraph to the next. They may appear in the middle of a paragraph to show two similar thoughts or to emphasize a thought that has been presented previously. Here are some useful transition words and phrases for main-idea-and-details essays.

> **To show similarities**
> likewise, like, similarly, similar to, as, also

> **To add to information that has been provided already**
> additionally, in addition, also, another, as well as, along with, besides, furthering this idea

> **To conclude**
> therefore, all in all, in conclusion, as has been shown, as you can see

Good Writing Tip: Repetition

Repetition, or restating critical information throughout an essay, promotes clarity, focus, and organization. It is useful to repeat your thesis statement at least once in an essay. Not only does this repetition remind readers of the main idea of the essay, it also helps to keep writers focused. Writers usually restate an essay's thesis in the concluding paragraph, but they may also combine a transition statement with a restatement of their thesis to ensure clarity, focus, and ultimately, organization.

Look back at the essay about humans' response to change on page 12. Find two transition statements, and explain each statement's purpose (to show similarities, to enhance given information, to conclude). Then identify the idea that is repeated in the essay.

Transition 1: _____ Purpose: _____

Transition 2: _____ Purpose: _____

Repeated idea: _____

Main Idea and Details *(continued)*

Application Read the three essay topics provided below. Then read the passage on page 16. When you finish reading the passage, choose one of the topics. You should choose the topic that either makes the most sense to you or that interests you the most, because you will be writing a main-idea-and-details essay based on this topic. Finally, remember that the topic you choose becomes the main idea of the essay you write.

Topics

1. Analyze the theme or controlling idea of "To Work or Not to Work, That Is the Question." What do you think the dominant message of this article is? Provide specific details from the text to support your answer.

2. Holding a job takes valuable time away from young people who need to focus on their studies in preparation for their futures. Write an essay clearly expressing this main idea, using details gathered from your reading and personal experience.

3. Holding a job teaches young people responsibility and prepares them for their futures in a way that sitting in a classroom cannot. Write an essay clearly expressing this main idea, using details gathered from your reading and personal experience.

Main Idea and Details (continued)

To Work or Not to Work, That Is the Question

At the age of fourteen, Pamela Sherwood began working. She made sundaes and dipped soft-serve cones at a local ice-cream stand. At first, Pamela worked twenty hours a week during the summer months. This reasonable schedule changed the next summer when Pamela discovered she could make more money working at a national ice-cream chain. The only problem was that Pamela would be hired only if she agreed to work throughout the summer as well as throughout the school year. Also, Pamela had to work at least thirty-five hours a week in the summer and at least fifteen hours a week during the school year. Thinking about all the money she would save for that new car she wanted and for her college education, Pamela accepted the offer. When Pamela's fifteenth birthday came in November, she couldn't even attend her own party because she was working. When report cards were issued, Pamela's grade point average had dropped from a respectable B to an alarming D+.

Pamela's situation is not unique. In American suburbia, teenagers are working long hours at nowhere jobs, often at the expense of their responsibilities as students; while young people's savings accounts may be increasing, the possibilities for their futures are decreasing because all of their energies are focused on work instead of school. Too often, young people do not realize that they are jeopardizing their futures by working long hours during the school year because the world of work is what they perceive to be their future.

Therefore, by earning a reputation as responsible, hardworking young people, teenagers think they are enhancing their future prospects. Unfortunately, college applications do not ask applicants how many satisfied customers they have served; rather, the applicant's academic performance and record are the deciding factors in whether an applicant is accepted or rejected from an academic institution.

So what is an ambitious young person to do? Unemployed teens are uncomfortably dependent on parents for financial support, while working teens are too tired to care about their day-to-day responsibilities, such as homework and studying. According to a 2001 study, 70 percent of teenagers are in the workforce. An alarming 66 percent of these teens work up to 57 hours per week. This is an amazing statistic as it shows that the majority of America's teens are working their lives away. What is even more disturbing about these numbers is that research shows that teens who work twenty or more hours a week are less enthusiastic about their futures, less motivated to earn high grades, and consequently receive lower grades than their nonworking peers. It should not come as a shock, then, to know that over the past few years there has been a 10 percent increase in summer-school enrollment. Sheila Keats, a high school math teacher who also teaches summer school, stated, "At the beginning of the summer-school session, I ask my students what went wrong during the school year. What made it so they could not pass their classes?

(continued)

Main Idea and Details (continued)

To Work or Not to Work, That Is the Question (continued)

Invariably, I get the same responses: 'I had to work and finding time to study was impossible, so I just didn't study.' Another common response is, 'By the time I get home from work, I'm too exhausted to do anything but go to sleep—I'm just too burned out to do my homework.'" This attitude—believing that work is a higher priority than school—is detrimental not only to the future of individual young people, but also to society as a whole. From where will the greatest American thinkers and innovators come if our young people are burned out by the age of sixteen?

Steps are being taken to decrease the risk of teen burnout. Some states, like Maryland, have passed laws making it illegal for teenagers to spend more than twelve hours a day at school and at work, and this includes time needed to complete homework assignments and projects and to study for tests and exams. Also, federal law forbids 14- to 16-year-olds to work more than three hours on school days, and they cannot work past 7 P.M. on school nights. Further still, some politicians are pushing a bill that, if made into law, would require school-age applicants to submit a transcript with their application. If the applicant's grades are below average, then she or he will not be hired. Despite these precautionary measures to protect young people from burnout and dropping out of school, teens continue to work their young lives away.

Not everything about young people and work is negative, though. Young workers learn to interact positively with a diverse group of people; they learn the importance of being on time, meeting expectations, and dressing appropriately. Additionally, young workers who work fewer than ten hours per week tend to have better time-management skills and are able to maintain their grades while enjoying a typical young person's social life—all while saving for that first car and college.

Perhaps the solution to the question of whether teens should work lies in the philosophy of Socrates, one of the greatest thinkers of the Western world. Socrates believed in moderation—in other words, too much of anything was never good. It seems as though this outlook applies nicely to working teens. Young people who let work consume their lives will not do well in school and in life. Young people who limit the amount of time they spend working to ten hours or less will do well in school and have enough energy left over to enjoy and succeed in life.

Main Idea and Details (continued)

Prewriting   **Brainstorming**

Brainstorm about the topic you chose. Change the web as needed.

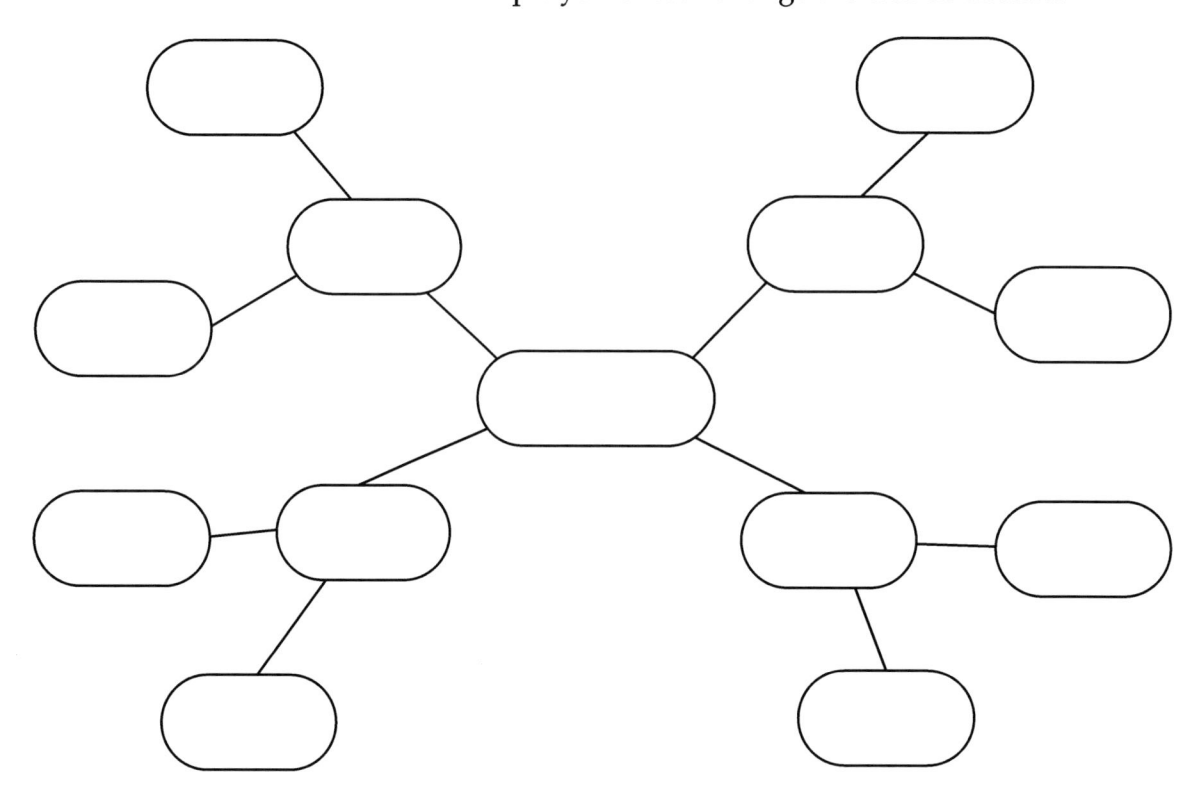

Narrow Your Topic

Now analyze your web. Then write your narrowed topic.

_____

Define Your Purpose

What do you want to show about your topic? Boil the purpose down into one sentence that you can use as a thesis statement.

_____

_____

Identify Your Audience

Write who your audience is and how this affects your writing.

_____

_____

Main Idea and Details *(continued)*

Drafting To clarify your ideas and organize your essay, fill in the graphic organizer below. Write your thesis statement—the main idea—in the top box. Then list the details that you will use to support your thesis statement. Add detail boxes as needed.

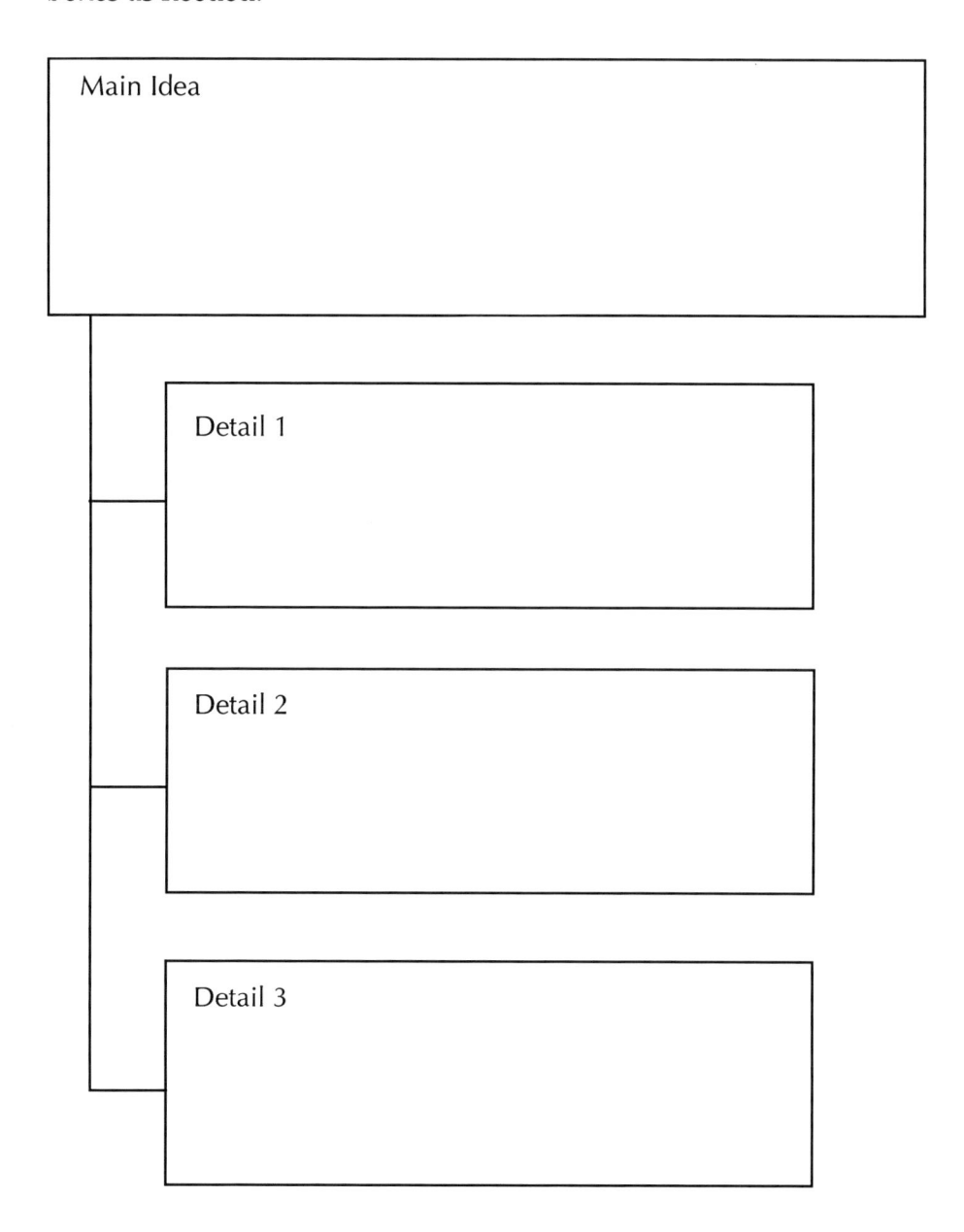

```
┌─────────────────────────────────┐
│ Main Idea                       │
│                                 │
│                                 │
└─────────────────────────────────┘
         │
         │     ┌───────────────────────────┐
         │     │ Detail 1                  │
         ├─────│                           │
         │     │                           │
         │     └───────────────────────────┘
         │
         │     ┌───────────────────────────┐
         │     │ Detail 2                  │
         ├─────│                           │
         │     │                           │
         │     └───────────────────────────┘
         │
         │     ┌───────────────────────────┐
         │     │ Detail 3                  │
         └─────│                           │
               │                           │
               └───────────────────────────┘
```

Now use the chart above to help you write the first draft of your essay on a separate sheet of paper.

Main Idea and Details *(continued)*

Revising and Publishing

Revising

A revision of an essay is exactly what it sounds like: a re-vision. Revising gives you the opportunity to look at the essay as a whole and add, delete, or change information as necessary. Revised essays are polished essays. Revised essays have something to say and say it in the clearest, most effective manner.

Your teacher can provide a general revising checklist to help you with this step of the writing process. Each writing assignment will pose different challenges, but this checklist gives you a place to begin. Keep in mind that the first pass at revising looks at the big picture. Later, you can attend to proofreading and technical details.

Ask Yourself Questions

For now, think about the ideas and organization of the essay. Ask yourself questions like the following. Use your answers to make changes to your essay.

Ideas
- Does the essay make sense?
- Is the main idea clear?
- Is the thesis statement well supported?
- Are the details specific?
- Do the details support the main idea, or do they get off track?
- Does the essay lead to a satisfying conclusion?
- Is the essay interesting?
- Does the essay meet its purpose?
- Does the essay address its intended audience?

Organization
- Does the conclusion parallel the introduction?
- Is the thesis statement echoed in the conclusion?
- Are the paragraphs arranged in an effective order?
- Are transitions used effectively?

Read Aloud

It may be helpful to read the essay aloud during the revising stage. Writers tend to overlook errors in their own writing. When you read the essay aloud, it is impossible to overlook errors, because you will hear them. Also, by reading your essay aloud, you will know if your writing makes sense. If it does not, you will stumble as you read.

Main Idea and Details (continued)

Peer Editing

Another method of revising that many writers find helpful is peer editing. This means that you share your first draft with a peer—someone who has the same writing assignment or who is in the same class—for feedback. Sometimes someone who is "in the same boat" will catch on to what you are trying to say and help you clarify it. In a peer-editing session, the writer tells the peer editor what she or he wants help with: organization, clarity, transitions, or whatever. The peer editor then reads the piece, looking out for the particular area in which the writer wants feedback. Your teacher can provide a peer-editing form to help with this process.

Now revise your first draft. When you have answered the big questions about the big picture, you'll move on to smaller questions.

Proofreading

The proofreading step of the revising process is where you take care of grammar, spelling, and punctuation. Your teacher can provide a proofreading checklist to help you with this step. If there are particular problem areas you are aware of in your writing, you may want to add those to the checklist.

Questions to ask yourself when you are concentrating on the small picture include

- Have I capitalized correctly?
- Have I spelled everything correctly?
- Have I punctuated correctly?
- Do subjects and verbs agree?
- Are the verb tenses consistent?
- Have I avoided fragments and run-on sentences?

Publishing

After you have polished the ideas and the way you communicated them, it is time to share your work.

Publishing means putting your writing in a form that can be shared. In school, this may mean writing your essay neatly in ink or word-processing it on a computer and printing it out. Your teacher will have guidelines about how the finished product should look and be presented.

Now publish your polished essay in a form acceptable to your teacher.

Lesson 8
Opinion and Supporting Evidence

Opinion An opinion is one person's thoughts about a specific topic. Opinions on their own are a dime a dozen; it does not take much brainpower or expertise to give an opinion.

Evidence What makes an opinion worthy of attention is supporting evidence—solid reasons that make the opinion reasonable. Think of an opinion as a featherless bird, and supporting evidence as feathers. Without the feathers, that bird cannot fly. But the more feathers it has, the higher and farther that bird can soar—and the more attention it will get.

If you asked someone their opinion about whether all children should be vaccinated against chicken pox, you might get some yes's and some no's. You might get some more passionate opinions such as "Of course, and any parent who doesn't have their child vaccinated should be arrested!" or "Absolutely not, and any parent who gives their child that vaccine should be arrested!"

Although the opinions may be valid to those who voice them, they carry no force—they have no support. If the people who answered said *why* they believe yes or no, the opinions would be more convincing.

Model Read the following opinion. What evidence is given for the opinion?

> When asked if they favored vaccinating children against chicken pox, all the pediatricians in the survey responded in the positive. Reasons included the small but real risk of serious complications from the disease, and the safety of the vaccine.

In this example, the opinion is that children should be vaccinated against chicken pox. The reasons are clearly stated: The disease can be dangerous, and the vaccine is safe. The opinion is given further weight by the fact that experts—in this case, pediatricians—share the opinion.

Opinion and Supporting Evidence (continued)

You could just as easily find support for the opposing viewpoint—that children should not be vaccinated against chicken pox. In fact, this is an ongoing debate. Both sides put forth their opinion and have evidence for it. The audience has to decide which argument is more convincing.

Fact Versus Opinion

When writing (or reading) an opinion and supporting evidence essay, it is important to be able to tell the difference between the opinion and the evidence. Facts give specific information that can be verified, or checked for truth. Facts often are stated in the form of statistics or other objective data. Facts are gleaned from reliable sources, such as recognized experts, reference books, and journals. Facts are considered facts when they are true for a great number of people, not just one. Facts do not change according to one's mood.

Opinion: I think Jenny's boots are cool!

Fact: Jenny's boots are black leather.

Try It

Read the passages below. As you read, keep in mind the difference between opinion and fact. After you have finished reading, answer the questions.

> *Passage A*
>
> What's all this talk about school uniforms and distractions in the classroom? News flash: Requiring uniforms will make kids hate school even more! Many of my friends use clothing for self-expression. Our sense of self would be utterly destroyed without freedom to dress as we choose. Students would probably find other, possibly destructive, ways to show individuality if we're all forced to wear khakis and loafers all the time. If school uniforms become required, I bet that violence will increase because of frustration, and test scores will go down. I think that requiring public school students to wear uniforms will cause more distractions because students will rebel.

Opinion and Supporting Evidence (continued)

Passage B

In March 2001, Massachusetts officials proposed a bill requiring all Massachusetts public school students to wear uniforms. The bill came about as a reaction to the increase in school violence and low standardized test results. The thinking behind this proposal is that students will focus their attention on their studies if there are fewer distractions in the classroom, and according to authorities, the clothing that students wear to classes causes considerable distractions.

The most ominous of these distractions are drugs and violence. A recent random telephone survey of 1,300 high school students revealed that 48% of students feel that drugs and violence are serious problems at their schools. Furthermore, a cooperative study between the National School Safety Center and the Centers for Disease Control shows that 24% of school violence is drug related and that 35% is gang related.

How do these problems relate to dress? Clearly, uniforms would limit the opportunities students have to stash away drugs and weapons, and gang members would be unable to distinguish themselves by dress if everyone wore the same outfit. For these reasons, Massachusetts officials believe that mandating uniforms will enhance the quality of education that students receive in public schools.

1. Which passage features more opinion than fact? _____

2. List some words that signal an opinion. _____

3. What evidence is given to support the opinion in passage B?_____
   _____

4. List the strengths of each passage.

   Passage A: _____

   Passage B: _____

Good Writing Tip: Use Strong Conclusion Words

You want to convince your audience that your opinion is the one they should agree with. Besides providing solid evidence, you can make your argument convincing by concluding with a bang.

Conclusion Words		
as a result	certainly	plainly
as evidenced by	clearly	surely
as the facts show	obviously	therefore
as you can see		

Opinion and Supporting Evidence (continued)

Application   Read the list of topics below. Then read the provided selections. After reading, you will write an opinion-and-supporting-evidence essay using one of the topics.

Topics

1. Humans, like cats, are curious beings. Sometimes the human imagination can get carried away. Do you think humans have let their imaginations get the best of them with regard to the giant squid, the Loch Ness monster, and extraterrestrials? Discuss your opinion, using support from the texts and from your own experience.

2. Truth is relative. What do you think is the truth behind the legends cited? You may focus on all three, or choose one or two. Discuss your opinion, using support from the texts and from your own experience.

3. It is arrogant to say that humans know all there is to know about life on Earth—and beyond. Earth's oceans and lakes, the universe, and what lies beyond the universe are all full of possibilities. Discuss the existence of the unknown. Do you believe that a giant squid, a monster in Loch Ness, and extraterrestrial life exist? You may focus on all three mysteries, or choose one or two. Discuss your opinion, using support from the texts and from your own experience.

The Giant Squid

What has an eye the size of an SUV hubcap, a razor-sharp birdlike beak that maims whatever it touches, eight sucker-lined arms, and a weight of one ton or more? The answer is the elusive *Architeuthis dux,* better known as the giant squid.

A member of the cephalopod family, the giant squid is one of nature's oldest marine mollusks. Its family tree reaches back 500 million years. Despite their gargantuan size and longevity, no human has ever seen one of these creatures alive and in its natural habitat. An obvious question, then, is, "Do these creatures really exist?" According to marine biologists, the answer is a resounding "Yes."

One of the earliest indicators that such a creature exists came in the form of a novel. Jules Verne, author of the 1870 science-fiction classic *20,000 Leagues Under the Sea,* got the idea for his famous deep-sea adventure from a navy report. The navy stated that one of its vessels had been attacked by a vicious eight-armed behemoth. Verne elaborated on this event, and the greatest sea monster of all time, the giant squid, was born. In the opening chapter Verne writes, "For some time past vessels had been met by 'an enormous thing,' a long object, spindle-shaped, occasionally phosphorescent, and infinitely larger and more rapid in its movements than a whale." More

(continued)

Opinion and Supporting Evidence (continued)

The Giant Squid (continued)

than a century later, scientists have little more proof of the giant squid's existence than Verne's fiction provides. Proof, however, does exist.

Sea crews and captains report sightings of sperm whales, the giant squid's presumed greatest enemy, with huge sucker scars on their bodies. Only one creature could cause such damage to such a large animal: the giant squid.

In addition, autopsies performed on sperm whales have revealed parts of huge squidlike creatures in the stomachs of the dead animals. Dying squids have been captured off the coast of Australia, the largest of which was a 26-foot-long female that weighed more than 1,100 pounds. Large squid carcasses have washed up on the shores of Australia, New Zealand, and, surprisingly, Massachusetts. These carcasses have been preserved and are on display at the Smithsonian Institute and the New York Museum of Natural History.

Still, none of these creatures comes close to the size of a bona fide giant squid. Furthermore, if giant squids as a group, rather than just large individual squids, exist, how have they escaped detection?

Researchers claim that its natural habitat has kept the true giant squid from human eyes. The giant squid inhabits the deepest part of the oceans, 3000 feet beneath the surface. Scientists have not yet mastered the technology required to send a human to such depths. Only unmanned submersibles have ever entered the dark, cold world of the giant squid. These vehicles are equipped with video cameras, but none has captured an image of the elusive and deadly cephalopod.

Marine biologists surmise that the animal travels at a sleek 45 miles per hour. To eat, it uses its two long tentacles, which are prehensile, or able to grasp. The captured prey then receives the "kiss of death," when the squid's massive beak tears into the victim's flesh. Female giant squids are believed to be larger than the males. Like its relative the octopus, the giant squid sprays thick, black ink when threatened.

Despite the lack of a living specimen or even a photographic image of one, marine biologists believe that the giant squid exists. Anecdotal, or oral, reports of strange sightings, the contents of dead whales' stomachs, and remains of larger-than-normal squids point to the existence of the giant squid. But for those to whom "seeing is believing," no hard evidence is available.

Opinion and Supporting Evidence *(continued)*

Nessie

It is the sixth century in the Scottish village of Drumnadrochit. Saint Columba has been summoned to Loch Ness to exorcise, or drive out, an otherworldy inhabitant. The saint arrives—and waits.

From the thick gray mist that hovers above Loch Ness, a long, thin, dark object emerges. A disproportionately small oval bobs at the tip; behind, three large, camellike humps break the surface of the murky lake. Then it disappears without a trace.

So goes the legend of the Loch Ness monster, also known as Nessie. There is some debate, however, over whether Saint Columba exorcised the creature from the loch, or exorcised fear of the creature from the villagers. Considering that there have been over ten thousand reported sightings of the alleged Loch Ness monster, the latter seems more likely. This leaves three possibilities. The first is that such a creature did exist in the loch, but Saint Columba drove it away. The second is that the saint merely rid the villagers of their fear, and the monster continues to exist. The third possibility is that the monster does not and never did exist. But what about all those sightings?

On the shore of Loch Ness sits the Drumnadrochit Hotel. In 1933, the owners reported seeing something rise from the lake—something the likeness and size of which had never before been seen. Shortly thereafter, every room in the hotel was full, and occupancy has not declined since then.

Loch Ness, located west of Scotland's Inverness, is the largest body of fresh water in the United Kingdom. It is eight hundred feet deep, twenty-four miles long, and one mile wide. The lake is dark and murky, and is not particularly rich in water life. In fact, some scientists claim that there is not enough food in the lake to sustain a creature the size of Nessie. The murkiness of the loch makes it difficult for researchers to pick up visual images beneath the water's surface. There have been instances, though, when the image of something large swimming in the depths has been captured on videotape. These include an image of what appears to be a large flipper, and a shot of what some believe to be the rear end of Nessie. Neither picture is conclusive, and both point toward the existence of sturgeon in Loch Ness, not necessarily a monster.

The evidence against Nessie's existence has increased over time. One famous 1934 photo of Nessie was revealed to be a hoax when a dying Christian Spurling, one of the men present when the picture was taken, confessed that the photograph had been rigged. Throughout the 1970s, photos of the Loch Ness monster appeared in the media, only to reappear later as the products of pranksters. Despite these revelations, many people continue to believe in Nessie. This is one of the hallmarks of legends: They never die.

Opinion and Supporting Evidence *(continued)*

Is All Well in Roswell?

In 1995, Fox Network aired what was listed in television schedules across the country as an alien autopsy. The ratings for this broadcast were through the roof. A bit later, Fox reaired the show, and again the ratings skyrocketed. You see, the program was advertised as a never-before-seen glimpse into the events of early July 1947, better known as the Roswell incident.

Roswell, New Mexico, is the home of desert, farmland, the Roswell Army Air Force base (RAAF), and the now-infamous Area 51. First there were reports of some sort of hovering aircraft that illuminated the night sky with shimmering lights. Then there was the crash.

Some folks say it was a newfangled weather balloon that crashed that July night more than fifty years ago. Others say it was a high-tech military spy plane. Still others claim that it was a flying saucer that slammed into the earth that summer evening.

On July 8, 1947, officials at RAAF issued a press release stating that the base had recovered the wreckage of a "flying disk." The quest for answers about the possible crash of an extraterrestrial aircraft was on.

The seeds of contention between believers in the ET theory and the nonbelievers were planted and flourish to this day. Those who believe that aliens crash-landed in Roswell also believe that officials for RAAF whisked away a surviving alien and then created an elaborate cover-up to lessen the public's fear and curiosity. The cover-up story involves a second press release rescinding, or withdrawing, the statements of the earlier press release. This second press release explained that the wreckage had been sent to a facility in Fort Worth, Texas, where it was determined to be the remains of a weather balloon. The press release addressed the surviving-alien rumor by saying that test dummies had been sent up in the balloon to test the effects of atmospheric pressure on human anatomy. The "alien" that had been recovered was just a test dummy.

The fiftieth anniversary of the crash brought with it renewed interest in the Roswell incident. RAAF officials, save one, state that the whole alien story was and is just a marketing ploy created by the Roswell Chamber of Commerce to attract tourists to the area. The holdout, Major Jesse Marcel, one of two military officials at the crash site in 1947, claimed that what he saw that night was a saucer. Marcel maintained this view throughout his life and took that belief to the grave.

The truth may never be known. What is known is that Fox Network undoubtedly made a tidy sum of money airing and reairing the alien autopsy show. Roswell does take in revenue from tourists and extraterrestrial aficionados who visit the area in hopes of adding to the Roswell saga. Perhaps money is the only reality necessary to perpetuate a myth.

Opinion and Supporting Evidence (continued)

Prewriting   **Brainstorming**

Brainstorm about the topic you chose. Change the web as needed.

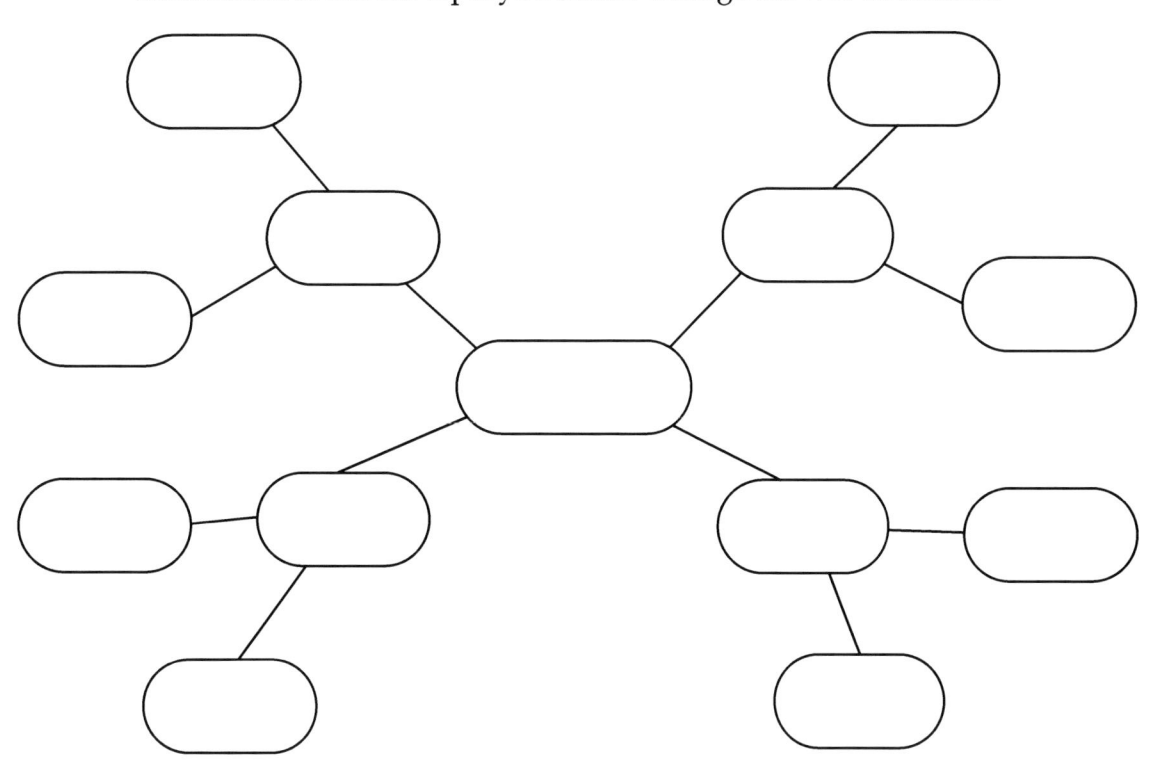

Narrow Your Topic

Now analyze your web. Then write your narrowed topic.

_____

Define Your Purpose

What do you want to show about your topic? Boil the purpose down into one sentence that you can use as a thesis statement.

_____

_____

Identify Your Audience

Write who your audience is and how this affects your writing.

_____

_____

Opinion and Supporting Evidence *(continued)*

Drafting Now that you have completed the prewriting process, you are ready to begin drafting. Use the graphic organizer below to plan and organize your essay. Start by writing your opinion. Then list the evidence that will persuade your readers to agree.

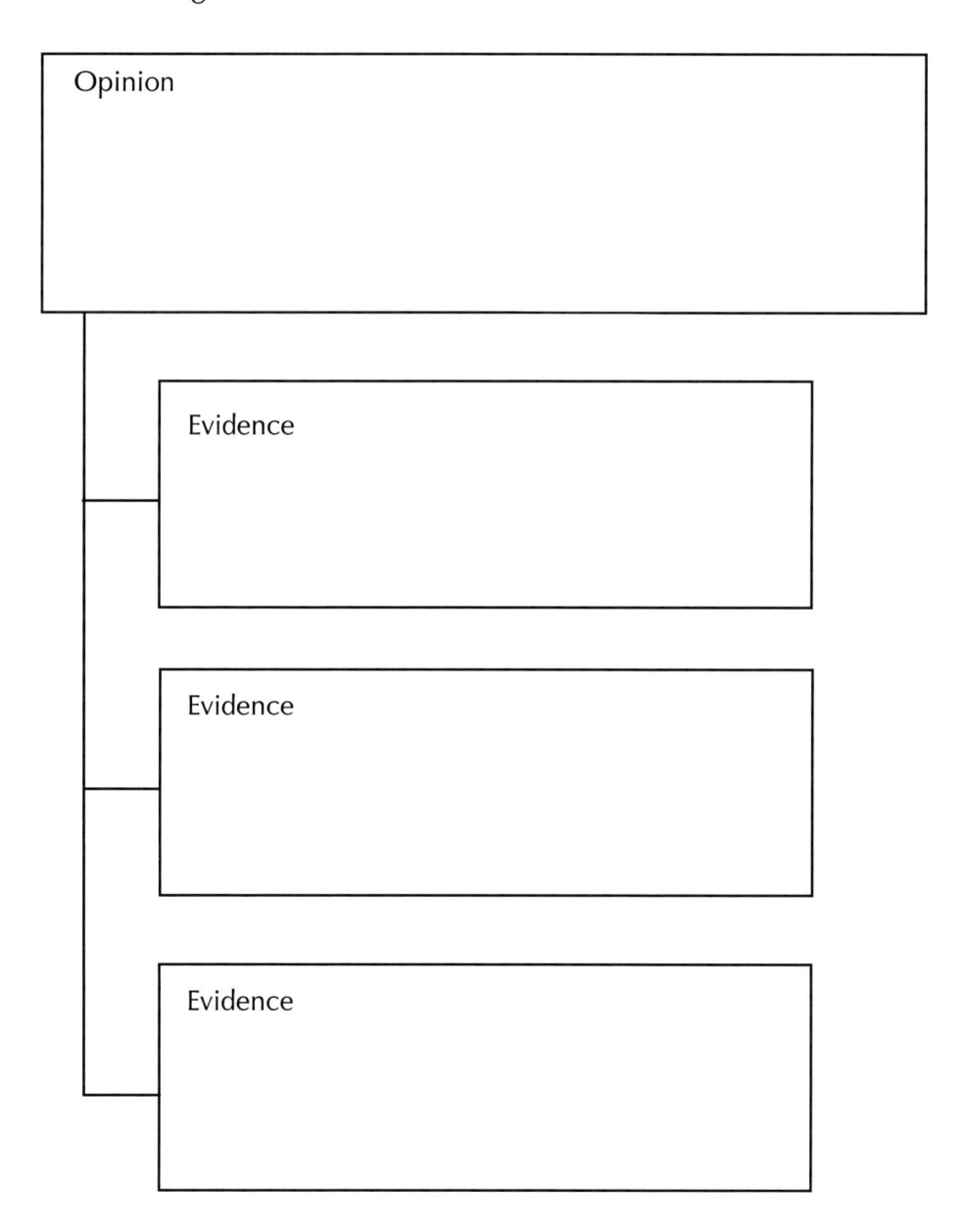

Opinion

Evidence

Evidence

Evidence

Use the graphic organizer above to help you write your first draft on another sheet of paper.

Opinion and Supporting Evidence (continued)

Revising and Publishing

Revising

Remember that the first pass at revision deals with the big issues. Ask yourself questions about the ideas and organization of your essay. Now read your work aloud to yourself.

You may want to ask yourself the following specific questions about your opinion-and-supporting evidence essay.

- Have I stated my opinion?
- Have I included enough evidence?
- Is the evidence reliable and believable?
- Have I used words that make clear what is opinion and what is fact?
- Have I used strong conclusion words?
- Have I arranged the evidence logically?

Peer Editing

You may want to ask a peer to be a sounding board and to comment on your essay. Your revising checklist from your teacher can also help by giving you general guidelines to follow. Now you can write your second draft.

Proofreading

After you have made your idea and organization revisions in your second draft, it is time to concentrate on the mechanics. Check for grammatical, spelling, and punctuation errors. Refer to your proofreading checklist from your teacher.

Publishing

When you are satisfied with your essay, publish it in a form acceptable to your teacher. Be sure your final draft is free of mistakes and is clear, clean, and easy to read. Create a title that will interest the reader.

Lesson 9
Compare and Contrast

When you **compare** and **contrast** subjects, you explore their similarities (compare) and differences (contrast). When you write a compare-and-contrast essay, you perform a side-by-side examination of two (or more) subjects. Your purpose may be to evaluate—to say that one subject is better than the other. Another purpose for comparing and contrasting is to explain the subjects by telling how they are similar and different.

Compare Imagine that you have been asked to write a compare-and-contrast essay about adventure movies and horror films. During the prewriting stage, you need to find points of comparison. These are things that your two subjects have in common. For the essay about movies, you might ask yourself, "What do these two types of films have in common?" You might answer, "They both have suspenseful plots, use special effects, and feature characters." These three items—plot, special effects, and characters—become the points of comparison in your essay.

Contrast The comparing step of finding points of comparison leads to the contrasting step. You tell what is different about those points for each subject. You might ask yourself, "What is different about the plots, special effects, and characters in these two types of movies?" After thinking about it, you might answer yourself, "The plots of both types require suspense and danger. Although what is being shown may differ, the special effects have to be dramatic for these types of films to live up to the expectations of thrills. But when it comes to characters, adventure movies usually have more rounded people whom the audience wants to see through to the end of the adventure, while horror movies often have stereotypical characters who are only there to be killed off."

Model Identifying the points of comparison and then the differences between your subjects can lead to a solid thesis statement. The following might serve as a thesis statement for the movie essay.

© 2002 J. Weston Walch, Publisher Content-Area Writing Strategies: Language Arts

Compare and Contrast (continued)

> Adventure movies and horror films both leave hearts pounding from the suspense and lungs gasping at the special effects, but when it comes to characters, adventure movies win hands down.

The essay with that thesis statement is clearly going to evaluate the two types of films. An essay that would explain the types of movies might have a thesis statement such as the following.

> Adventure movies and horror movies are both meant to thrill and excite the viewer, but the characters serve different purposes in each. In adventure movies, the audience wants the characters to survive their adventure; in horror movies, many characters are intended *not* to survive theirs.

Organization Once you have identified the similarities and differences between your subjects, you have to decide how you want to organize your compare-and-contrast essay. There are two choices: subject by subject, or point by point. In the subject-by-subject organization, you discuss Subject A as a whole, then you discuss Subject B. A blueprint of that essay might look something like this.

ADVENTURE MOVIES (Subject A)
Plot
Special effects
Characters

HORROR MOVIES (Subject B)
Plot
Special effects
Characters

In a point-by-point organization, you deal with both subjects at once but focus on one point of comparison at a time. That essay might look like this.

PLOT
Adventure movies (Subject A)
Horror movies (Subject B)

SPECIAL EFFECTS
Adventure movies (Subject A)
Horror movies (Subject B)

CHARACTERS
Adventure movies (Subject A)
Horror movies (Subject B)

Compare and Contrast (continued)

Whether you are evaluating or explaining, writing subject by subject or point by point, it is important to arrange your ideas effectively. Often, writers choose to start with their most important ideas and move to their least important. The reverse can also work. Either way, it makes sense to progress logically, rather than to jump around between points of varying importance or strength.

Good Writing Tip: Use Transitions

Certain transitional words can signal comparisons and contrasts. Use such words to show the relationships among your ideas.

Compare Words	
also	like
and	likewise
another	moreover
as well as	similarly
in the same way	too
just as	

Contrast Words	
although	instead
as opposed to	nevertheless
but	on the other hand
conversely	
despite	still
however	unlike
in contrast	while
in spite of	yet

Try It

Read the article below. Then answer the questions that follow.

Haiku and Jengo: One Cat and One Dog

Haiku, a sleek gray kitty, enters the television room oblivious to the group of five people who are talking animatedly about the program. Her nose is poised high in the air as she saunters to the very center of the room and settles down in front of the television, her back to the group. In stark contrast to Haiku's dignified and calculated entrance is that of Jengo, a young bullmastiff who is all ears, legs, and muzzle. Jengo blusters into the room like a gust of wind, his frantically wagging tail knocking over soda cans and bowls of pretzels. Like Haiku, Jengo waggles his way to the very center of the room, but unlike Haiku, Jengo faces his human audience, eager for attention. There they sit, Haiku and Jengo, both desiring the presence of people, yet expressing their desires in different manners.

Cats are independent animals who are much more comfortable slinking around in tall grass than they are chasing Frisbees at the park. Cats, at their core, are predators who coolly classify everything as prey or not prey. They are calculating observers rather than participants. Dogs, on the other hand, are very social animals that depend on humans for a sense of purpose. They thrive on interaction with others, and

(continued)

Compare and Contrast (continued)

Haiku and Jengo: One Cat and One Dog (continued)

perceive life as a big playground full of opportunity for fun. Dogs are eager to please humans, and can be a bit excessive when showing affection. Cats can be affectionate, too, but they usually reserve their attentions until they are in the mood.

As pets, cats and dogs provide their owners with various benefits and rewards. Studies show that cats reduce their owners' stress level and lower their blood pressure just by being nearby and purring. Also, cats are fastidious animals that enjoy cleanliness; cats keep themselves fresh and do their best to maintain a neat living area. What's more, cats do away with intruding vermin, such as mice, creating a pest-free environment for their owners. Similarly, dogs aid in reducing their owners' stress levels and lowering their blood pressure, but this benefit comes only when the dogs behave. Dogs are more likely than cats to become anxious when their owners leave for school or work, and this anxiety can result in destructive behaviors. Wooden doorframes riddled with teeth marks, bedspreads that are torn to shreds, and household items chewed beyond recognition and strewn throughout the house are some traces of the ways in which a dog expresses anxiety. Clearly, coming home to such devastation would do anything but lower stress and reduce blood pressure. Dogs, however, provide their owners with companionship and protection in a way that cats do not. For example, dogs can be trained to perform tricks that entertain their owners; cats, while intelligent enough to be trained to do tricks, prefer not to be. And this, perhaps, sums up the greatest difference between cats and dogs: Cats do only what they want to do; dogs, for the most part, do what they think will please their owners.

Disgusted by Jengo's clumsy friendliness, Haiku leaps from her spot on the floor to the top of the television; from take-off to landing, her motion is streamlined and flawless. She faces her audience with an air of superiority. Meanwhile, Jengo has begun to yelp, excited by Haiku's movement. As their owner hurriedly removes Jengo from the room, Haiku is swept up lovingly into someone's arms where she is pampered and stroked for as long as she sees fit.

1. List the compare words and the contrast words from the article above.

2. How is this essay arranged: subject by subject, or point by point?

3. Is this essay intended to evaluate, or to explain? Why do you think so?

Compare and Contrast *(continued)*

Application Read the three essay topics below. Then read the provided passages. When you finish reading the passages, choose one of the essay topics. You should choose the topic that either makes the most sense to you or that interests you the most, for you will be writing a cause-and-effect essay based on this topic.

Topics

1. Focus on the differences between distance runners and those who play on teams. Base your response on the information given in the articles; you may add information from personal experience to enhance your response.

2. Focus on the similarities between distance runners and those who play on teams. What makes a distance runner comparable to a team player? Base your response on the information given in the articles; you may add information from personal experience to enhance your response.

3. Focus on your experience as either a distance runner or a team player. (Base your response on one of the articles below, depending on your personal experience.) How does your experience compare with those presented in articles below? Is your experience similar to that described below, or is it vastly different? Part of your response will be based on the information given in one of the articles; personal experience will serve as the source for the other part.

The Solitude of the Distance Runner

If you asked Joan Benoit Samuelson, Uta Pepig, or Greta Weitz, all world-class distance runners, whom they hold responsible for winning a race or losing a race, their answers would be the same. Each would say with conviction, "I am responsible for a win or a loss."

Regardless of the distance of the race—five kilometers, ten kilometers, a marathon—distance runners know that winning or losing is completely up to them. There is no teammate to pass the ball to, nor is there a goalkeeper to fend off an approaching opponent. When you are a distance runner, all you have is your will and your skill.

Distance runners' training regime requires dogged perseverance and an ironclad will. Runners awake in the morning, don their running clothes, lace up their running shoes, stretch, and hit the pavement for an hour or two of endurance training, also known as aerobic training, before the average person has hit the snooze button on the alarm clock. Most runners adore this part of their training regimen because of the control they have over their workout. The pace at which they run, the route they follow, and the distance of that route is determined by no one but them. Also, running seven miles or fifteen miles, even a quick

(continued)

Compare and Contrast (continued)

The Solitude of the Distance Runner

three miles, allows runners to dig deep inside to get in touch with their true ability. Can I take this hill a little faster? Can I run this last mile in under five minutes, thirty seconds? Can I sprint these last two hundred yards? As the runner comes closer to the end of her run, she checks her runner's watch and notices that, if she pours it on for the remainder of the run, she will better her time for this particular route, creating a new personal best. She pumps her arms faster; her leg speed increases automatically, to keep pace with her arms. Her breathing quickens, as does her heart rate. She sees the imaginary finish line, and increases her pace until she sprints, full speed, past the imaginary line, twenty-five seconds ahead of her best time. No crowds are there to cheer for her personal victory; there are no teammates with whom she can celebrate. Only the rising sun and the quiet morning are present to celebrate this victory. But for runners everywhere, professional or recreational, young or old, male or female, shaving twenty-five seconds off a personal best time and still feeling strong enough to sprint past the finish line is reward enough.

Another alluring aspect of distance running is its peacefulness. If they run in the early morning or later in the evening, runners can listen to the rhythms their bodies create. A heartbeat becomes a metronome, encouraging the arms and legs to pump faster and faster. Footfalls become a drumbeat that quickens and slows depending on the song the runner is listening to inside his mind. Breathing is an internal lullaby that distributes the runner's fuel, precious oxygen, throughout the body. Such unity of mind, body, and soul is difficult to come by in other sports.

During competition, runners visualize leaving the starting line with lightning speed, determined to be spared the confusion and stutter steps that come with a slow start, and then settling into a comfortably fast pace, which is often referred to as finding one's rhythm. Once a runner has found his rhythm, he must begin to steadily and mercilessly close the gap between himself and anyone who happens to be in front of him. Doing so requires the skill and will mentioned earlier. First, the runner sets his sights on his opponent and matches the opponent's foot speed, or turnover rate. Steadily, he begins to build upon his opponent's pace, sneaking in two steps to his opponent's one. As the gap between the two begins to close, the runner positions himself behind his opponent just off his opponent's right shoulder, and settles into his opponent's pace. This is called "drafting"; the runner places himself in a position to draft off his opposition. In other words, the runner lets his opponent remain in the lead position so it is the opponent who is doing all of the hard work, like cutting into the wind. This allows the runner to use his opposition as a shield until he has saved up enough energy to pass the person off whom he has been drafting. When passing his opponent, the runner must

(continued)

Compare and Contrast (continued)

The Solitude of the Distance Runner (continued)

maintain a strong and quick pace until he is fifty yards ahead. Passing with conviction intimidates opponents, as they feel there is no way that they are going to be able to overtake the runner who has passed them. Once again, a runner's will and skill, and nothing else, leads him to victory.

All aspects of distance running require an aptitude for solitude. From practice to competition, a runner has no one to depend upon except for herself. Such independence and focus on the self for motivation and inspiration is rare in sports and is exactly what sets distance runners apart from other athletes.

There's No "I" in "Team"

Being a member of a team requires members to place individual needs, wants, and expectations second to those of the team. Someone who is selfish and seeks personal glory alone will hinder a team's progress.

In the 2000–2001 National Basketball Association (NBA) season, stories of conflict between Los Angeles Lakers' stars Kobe Bryant and Shaquille O'Neil made sports headlines nearly every day. The veteran O'Neil was upset by the number of times Bryant had his hands on the ball. O'Neil complained that Bryant was "hogging" the basketball. Instead of focusing on the amazing talent of the Lakers team as a whole, the focus was on the apparent selfishness of its individual players. This is not what team sports are all about. Team sports are based on the unity and equality of all team members. Of course, there are some players who are more talented and effective than others, but it is the unity of the team as a whole that wins games.

The importance of a team's ability to work together shines through during practices. First, a practice cannot begin until all team members are present and ready to work, learn, and sweat together. The team captains lead the team through a series of stretches and calisthenics in preparation for the demands the practice session will place on their bodies and their minds. Usually there is a lot of chanting, clapping, and cheers of encouragement throughout this preparation period. If an individual is feeling sluggish or a bit worn out physically, the team's verbal encouragement will inspire him to persevere. The enthusiasm of the team as a whole will motivate those whose minds may not be focusing on the task at hand. Also, an individual who is having a bad day will find comfort in the presence of his teammates, who will do everything in their power to help lift his spirits. On successful teams, individual players never feel alone, and they know that they can rely on their teammates for encouragement and motivation.

Once the warm-up session is done, the rigorous part of the practice begins. Typically, this portion of a practice can last from two to four hours and usually involves aerobic exercise, such as running laps, to enhance individuals' endurance. Anaerobic exercise,

(continued)

Compare and Contrast (continued)

There's No "I" in "Team" (continued)

such as wind sprints and "suicides," involve a series of short sprints, the length of which increase with each repetition, to increase individuals' speed and reaction time. Skills-based exercise, such as scrimmages and technique circuit drills, enhance individuals' dexterity, agility, and effectiveness on the field or on the court.

In addition to improving individual prowess and ability, this part of the practice teaches team members how to communicate and work effectively with each other. Basketball, football, soccer, field hockey, lacrosse, and many other team sports require members to know exactly where their teammates are at all times so they can advance the ball with lightning speed and without hesitation. Movement up and down the field must be synchronized and seamless. The concentration and awareness required of members of a team is unsurpassed in any other arena.

Team morale remains high naturally because, regardless of the intensity and length of a practice session or a game, members know that they are not the only ones who are pushing themselves to the limit. This camaraderie among teammates keeps the team unified and motivated.

Complementing a team's morale is the presence of fans or spectators. Oftentimes, spectators come to watch a team practice to lend their support and appreciation. This inspires team members to work hard throughout the practice session, because they know people are watching them, care about their progress, and obviously appreciate their hard work. Of course, spectator support carries over into game situations and provides the team with an indescribable feeling of importance and invincibility.

There's really no better feeling in the world than that of being a member of a winning team. To be a winning team, however, individual members must make their personal objectives secondary to the team's objectives, allowing the truism "There is no 'I' in team" to become a reality.

Compare and Contrast *(continued)*

Prewriting   **Brainstorming**

Use this web to brainstorm about your topic. Change the web as needed.

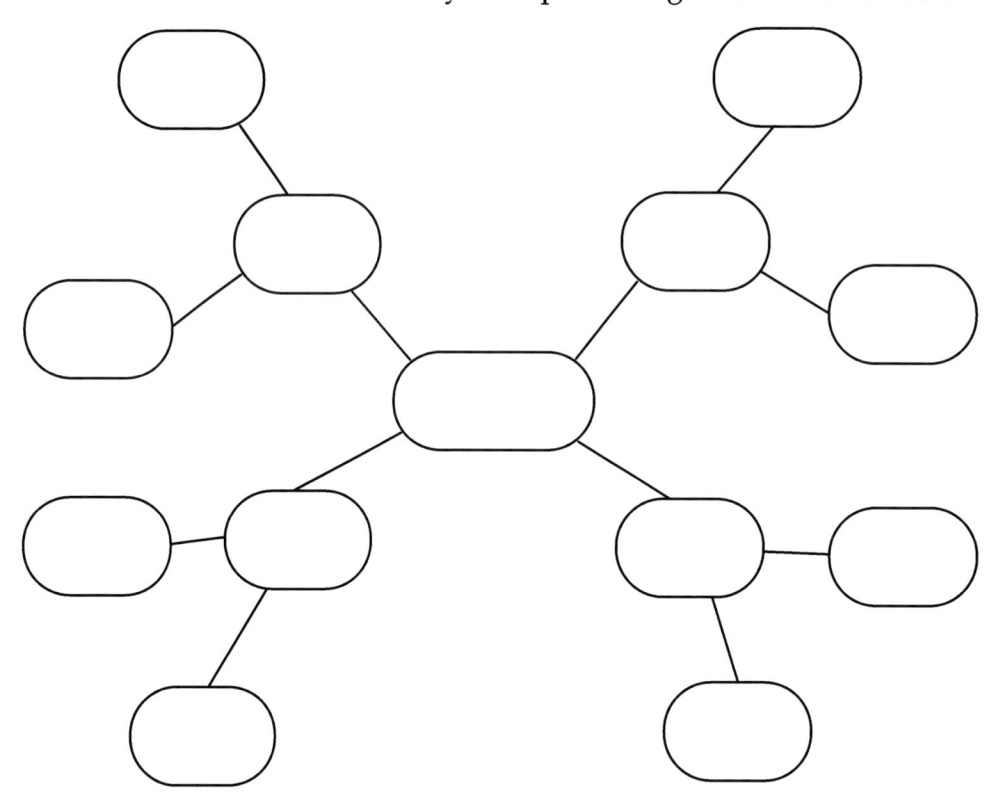

Narrow Your Topic

Now analyze your web to narrow your topic. Write your narrowed topic.

_____

Define Your Purpose

Think about your purpose for writing this essay. Write your purpose in one clear sentence. This can become your thesis statement.

_____

_____

Identify Your Audience

Write who your audience is and how this affects your writing.

_____

_____

Compare and Contrast *(continued)*

Drafting Use the graphic organizer below to help you write the first draft of your compare-and-contrast essay. This graphic organizer is called a Venn diagram.

You may remember the Venn diagram from math class. It is made up of two intersecting ovals. Where the ovals overlap, you write what the two subjects have in common. Where the ovals do not overlap, you write how the subjects are different.

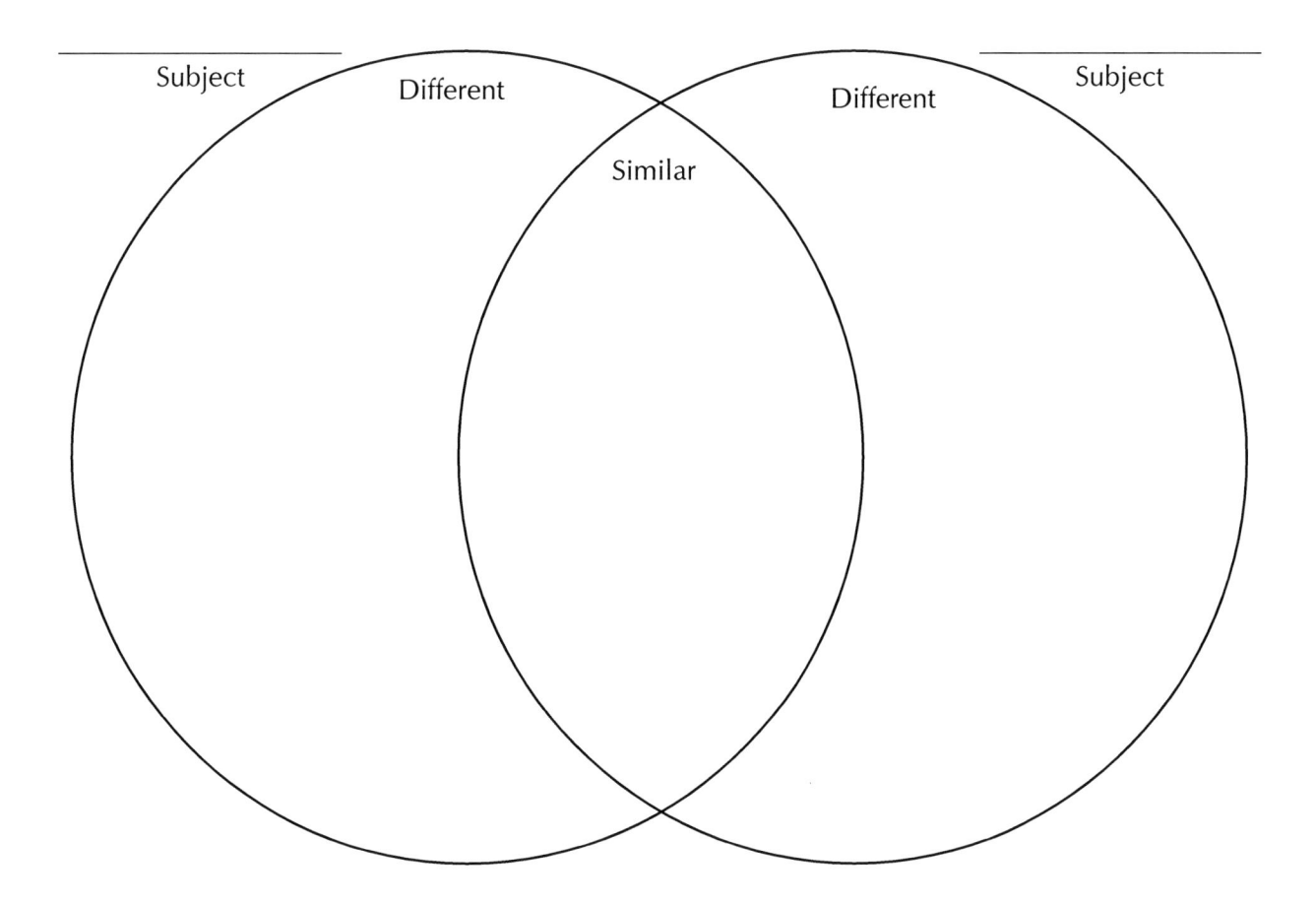

_____   _____
Subject   Different   Different   Subject

                              Similar

Now write the first draft of your essay on a separate sheet of paper.

Compare and Contrast (continued)

Revising and Publishing

Revising

Reread your first draft, looking for places where your ideas and organization can be improved. Some questions you may want to ask yourself about your compare-and-contrast essay include the following:

- Are my subjects clear?
- Have I written a clear thesis statement that shows why I am comparing and contrasting these things?
- Have I progressed logically in my comparison/contrast?
- Have I used compare words and contrast words?

Peer Editing

You may want to ask a peer to be a sounding board and to comment on your essay. Your revising checklist from your teacher can also help by giving you general guidelines to follow. Now you can write your second draft.

Proofreading

After you have made your idea and organization revisions in your second draft, it is time to concentrate on the mechanics. Check for grammatical, spelling, and punctuation errors. Refer to your proofreading checklist from your teacher.

Publishing

After you have polished your essay, publish it in a form acceptable to your teacher. Be sure your final draft is clean, clear, and easy to read. Create a title that captures the reader.

Lesson 10
Cause and Effect

A common pattern of organization in almost any field is cause and effect. A cause, or reason, leads to an effect, or result. An essay in this pattern shows how or why things happen. A book report might explain how one plot event caused another. A character sketch might explain how a character's experiences led to a certain behavior. You might see this pattern in a news story about a battle or a new law, for example. A story about a new medical treatment might explain how the drug attacks the disease. A sports article might tell why one team won over another. A math text might explain how you arrive at an answer. All these can be presented in the cause-and-effect pattern.

There may be multiple causes and multiple effects in one situation. For example, "Black ice made me lose control of the car" shows one cause—black ice—and one effect—loss of control. Another sentence might give more than one cause for the same effect: "Black ice and low visibility contributed to the accident." Similarly, one cause may lead to more than one effect: "The crash wrecked the car and broke my arm."

Even though a cause must come before the effect in real time, it does not have to come before the effect in writing. The sentence "We crashed the car after sliding on black ice" still shows the cause-and-effect relationship, but the effect is told first, followed by an explanation, the cause.

Model

When you write a cause-and-effect essay, you may focus on a cause or causes, an effect or effects, or a combination.

For example, imagine that you are going to write about Nomar Garciaparra, the Red Sox shortstop. To discuss the athlete's widespread popularity, you might write an introductory paragraph like the following.

> Nomar Garciaparra is an outstanding athlete; there is no debate about it. But there are many fine sports stars who, while respected for their abilities, are not beloved. Why is Nomar Garciaparra so popular? It is his interactions with others, his generosity, and his down-to-earth attitude that endear him to the public.

In the opening paragraph about Nomar Garciaparra, the cause-and-effect relationship is made clear. The question *why* asks for the causes leading to a

Cause and Effect (continued)

specific effect—Garciaparra's popularity. The answer appears in the thesis statement, the last line of the introduction.

In a different essay, you might be asked to write about the effects of an athlete's popularity, as in the following example.

> Yankee Derek Jeter is known as a nice guy and, of course, a great athlete. This popularity translates into benefits not only for him, but for others as well. Attendance at Yankees games is up, pleasing the owners. The team is well regarded by the public and other professionals, making the players and fans happy. And today's kids have someone worthy to look up to, a bonus for all of society.

Good Writing Tip: Do Not Oversimplify

If you oversimplify, your readers will not find your essay believable. Or they may believe you once, but not again if your explanations turn out to be untrue. Be sure to use well-researched causes and effects. Be able to show that the two truly are related, not just coincidental. For example, imagine that you are a reporter writing about an office full of workers who got sick after a new air conditioner was installed. To be sure it was the air conditioner that caused the illness, you would have to investigate other possible reasons. If you interviewed the workers and found that all the sick people had also eaten at the same restaurant, the cause of the illness might not be the new air conditioner. If you said it was, you might be wrong.

Good Writing Tip: Use Signal Words

Some words alert the reader to cause-and-effect relationships. Such words make it easier to follow your essay. They make the relationships between events clearer.

> **Cause-and-Effect Words**
> after
> as a consequence
> as a result
> because
> following x, y happened
> since
> then
> x led to y

Cause and Effect (continued)

Try It Read the cause-and-effect article below. Think about what effect is being investigated, and what the causes are. After you have finished reading, answer the questions that follow.

Baseball caps, oftentimes worn backward. Baggy jeans with fringed cuffs dragging on the pavement. Low, loose waistbands allowing for a peek at striped boxers. Customized Adidas without laces. Personalized Nikes without heels. Where do fashion designers get these outlandish fashion ideas? From kids just like you, that's where.

Highly recognizable clothes designers, such as Calvin Klein, Tommy Hilfiger, and the Gap, as well as footwear designers, such as Adidas and Nike, use teens and preteens to guide their latest fashion creations. This is how new styles happen. Fashion scouts are hired by designers to observe kids and how they dress. The fashion scouts' objective is to seek out the most unique and promising fashion trends. Because New York City and Los Angeles tend to be where trends start, scouts usually begin their search for the latest styles at malls, skateboard parks, movie theaters, and other places in these two famed cities where kids congregate.

The hip-hop look, which features the above-mentioned baseball caps, baggy jeans, and an inch or two of the wearer's boxers, first appeared on MTV on artists like the Beastie Boys and the late Tupac Shakur. Teens and preteens in New York City were quick to adopt this loose style. Fashion scouts, of course, picked up on this trend and reported back to the designers, who quickly began making oversized jeans and marketing them to kids. As a result, the hip-hop trend exploded in the late 1990s and variations of this look continue to pop up in high-end stores across the country.

One of these hip-hop inspired looks is the laceless and heelless sneaker. Scouts in California observed kids walking around with their Adidas untied; other times, kids removed the laces from the shoe altogether. This observation led to laceless slip-on sneakers. Nike's heelless sneaker was inspired by a group of New York teens who were spotted walking around a Soho skateboard park with their feet not fully in their shoes; their heels, crushing down the heels of their shoes, created a kind of sneaker-clog. Nike's scouts reported this behavior to their designers, and voilà, the heelless sneaker was born.

Only the biggest names in the fashion world can say what the next fashion statement will be, but who knows, maybe you and your friends will start the next fashion craze.

Cause and Effect (continued)

1. What is the main effect that is explored in this essay? There are several, but, right now, look for the main effect that controls the content of the essay.

2. What is the main cause behind the above effect? Again, there are many causes discussed in the essay, but look for the one main cause that leads directly to the main effect.

3. List at least three other effects in the essay.

4. List the causes for the effects you listed in number 3.

5. List the cause-and-effect words in the essay.

Application Read the list of essay topics, then read the provided passages. When you finish reading the passages, choose one of the topics with which to work. You should choose the topic that either makes the most sense to you or that interests you the most. You will use this topic to write a cause-and-effect essay.

Topics

1. Throughout his long journey from Troy to his home in Ithaca, Odysseus encounters many beings that teach him valuable life lessons. Becoming a better person is the effect Odysseus' journey has on him. After reading about his journey, choose two adventures and show how they led Odysseus to be a more humble, modest, and patient man.

2. Discuss the two adventures that cause Odysseus to be a wiser decision maker and man.

3. Read about Odysseus' experiences before, during, and after his journey home to Ithaca. Explain the effect the journey has on Odysseus' relationship with the gods.

Cause and Effect (continued)

Odysseus and the Trojan War

After ten long years of battling with the Trojans, Odysseus, the Greek King of Ithaca, comes up with an idea that, if executed correctly, would win the war for the Greeks. Using wood from the thousand ships that had sailed from Greece to Troy, Odysseus and his men create the Trojan Horse, a hollow structure large enough to hide all of the Greeks inside its mammoth body.

After the difficult task of convincing the Trojans to accept the horse as a peace offering—something that never would have been accomplished without the assistance of Poseidon, god of the sea and earthquakes—the horse is brought inside the walls of Troy. When all the Trojans are sleeping after their victory celebration, Odysseus and his men climb out from the hollow belly of the horse and attack the unsuspecting Trojans.

The Greeks declare victory, and Odysseus boasts to the gods that he and he alone vanquished the Trojans. Thus begins Odysseus' tempestuous journey homeward.

Deceitful Men

Odysseus and his men, who are divided evenly among twelve ships, come upon Ismarus, a stronghold for the Cicones. Here Odysseus and his men sack the Cicones, and Odysseus orders his men to take any wine and food that they may need and to hurry aboard their ships. Odysseus' men do not listen to him and, against Odysseus' orders, revel in the abundance of meat and tasty liquor that the Cicones' have had to sacrifice to them. While Odysseus' men waste time, however, the Cicones gather reinforcements and counterattack. In the end, Odysseus loses six men from each of his ships, and sails from Ismarus saddened by his men's betrayal and his losses.

Much later in Odysseus' journey, his men betray him again, and the punishment is much more dire. Odysseus and his men land upon the island of Thrinacia, home of Hyperion, god of the sun. Hyperion breeds sacred cattle, which must not be harmed by anyone. Odysseus has been warned not to touch Hyperion's cattle, and he has told his men as much, but Odysseus' men are starving and decide to ignore Odysseus' warning. While Odysseus is praying to the gods, his men slaughter Hyperion's sacred cattle. Hyperion calls upon Zeus to avenge the wrong that has been done to him, and Zeus obliges by sending down lightning bolts that destroy all of Odysseus' ships and men. Odysseus is the only survivor.

Ogres

Odysseus and his men encounter flesh-eating monsters throughout their journey homeward. One of these ogres is Polyphemus, King of the Cyclopes and son of Poseidon. While Polyphemus is away from his home, which is a gigantic cave, Odysseus and his men decide to make themselves comfortable inside the cyclops' cave. Odysseus hopes that the person who lives in the cave will offer his men and him some hospitality. Plus, Odysseus wants to see the huge being that resides in the cave.

(continued)

Cause and Effect (continued)

Odysseus and the Trojan War (continued)

Polyphemus returns, and Odysseus and his men are disgusted by his ugliness. He has one eye, is gigantic in size, and is just plain homely! Polyphemus is not happy to see intruders in his home and decides to eat two of Odysseus' men for dinner. Odysseus is horrified and enraged—as are his men—at this barbaric act and wants to kill Polyphemus. But Odysseus knows he can't kill the cyclops yet. A huge boulder serves as a door to the cave, and Polyphemus is the only one who is strong enough to move it. Since Polyphemus placed the boulder in front of the cave's opening when he came in, if Polyphemus is killed, Odysseus and his men will be trapped inside the cave forever. So Odysseus must be patient and wait until he has a plan that will injure Polyphemus, but not kill him.

Odysseus does come up with a plan, but not before Polyphemus snacks on more of Odysseus' men. Knowing he has to act quickly to save the rest of his men, Odysseus offers Polyphemus a huge bowlful of potent wine. The greedy Polyphemus drinks bowl upon bowl of this wine, until he is too intoxicated to keep his eye open. The giant cyclops passes out, and Odysseus and his men get to work.

First, Odysseus and his men blind Polyphemus by sharpening Polyphemus' shepherd's stick and jabbing it into the ogre's eye. Then, when Polyphemus lets his sheep out to graze, Odysseus and his men escape by hanging on to the undersides of the animals.

As they sail away from Polyphemus' island, Odysseus brags of his escape, exclaiming, "If anyone asks who has blinded you, tell them it was I, the mighty Odysseus, King of Ithaca!"

Polyphemus calls upon his father, Poseidon, to avenge the damage that Odysseus and his men inflicted on him.

*****

The beautiful sorceress Circe warns Odysseus of two more ogres, Scylla and Charybdis, that inhabit the two sides of a strait that Odysseus and his men must sail through to reach their destination. Circe tells Odysseus that he will be better off sailing closer to Scylla than passing too close to Charybdis. Odysseus must decide by which ogre he will pass.

Scylla is a six-headed, six-necked, twelve-footed, flesh-tearing monster that devours six men at a time. Charybdis is a violent whirlpool that devours ships full of men in one gigantic gulp. Without telling his men what they are about to encounter in case they panic, Odysseus directs his men to pass by Scylla's side of the strait. Out of nowhere, Scylla strikes, gobbling up one of Odysseus' men for each of her heads. Six men are lost because of Odysseus' decision; however, many more men survive.

Odysseus Returns Home

When Odysseus finally arrives home in Ithaca, he learns that hundreds of men have been harassing his beautiful and faithful wife Penelope, forcing her

(continued)

Cause and Effect *(continued)*

Odysseus and the Trojan War (continued)

to choose one of them as a husband. Also, Odysseus learns that these same men plan to kill his son, Telemachus. Full of rage, Odysseus wants immediate revenge on all who have wronged him, his wife, and his son. However, before he lashes out in violence, Odysseus realizes that he must learn who has been faithful to him so that he does not harm innocent people. Athena, the goddess of wisdom and Odysseus' guardian, assists Odysseus, disguising him as an old beggar. In this disguise, Odysseus is able to observe those who deserve to be punished and those who deserve to be spared. Odysseus reveals his identity to Telemachus, his son, and the two work together to rid Ithaca of those who have mistreated Odysseus' family and estate.

The day of reckoning comes, and Odysseus reveals himself to his enemies. All the wrongdoers are killed at the hands of Odysseus, Telemachus, and two loyal servants.

Upon seeing that all the men who acted so horribly year after year have been killed, one of Odysseus' servants cries out in joy. Odysseus, now a changed man, tells this servant not to rejoice over others' deaths, for it is not wise, nor is it honorable, to boast and brag about the loss of life, regardless of whether it is deserved or not. Odysseus tells his servant to celebrate in silence in honor of the gods who can either grant life or take it away at will.

Cause and Effect (continued)

Prewriting   **Brainstorming**

Brainstorm using the web below. Change the web as needed.

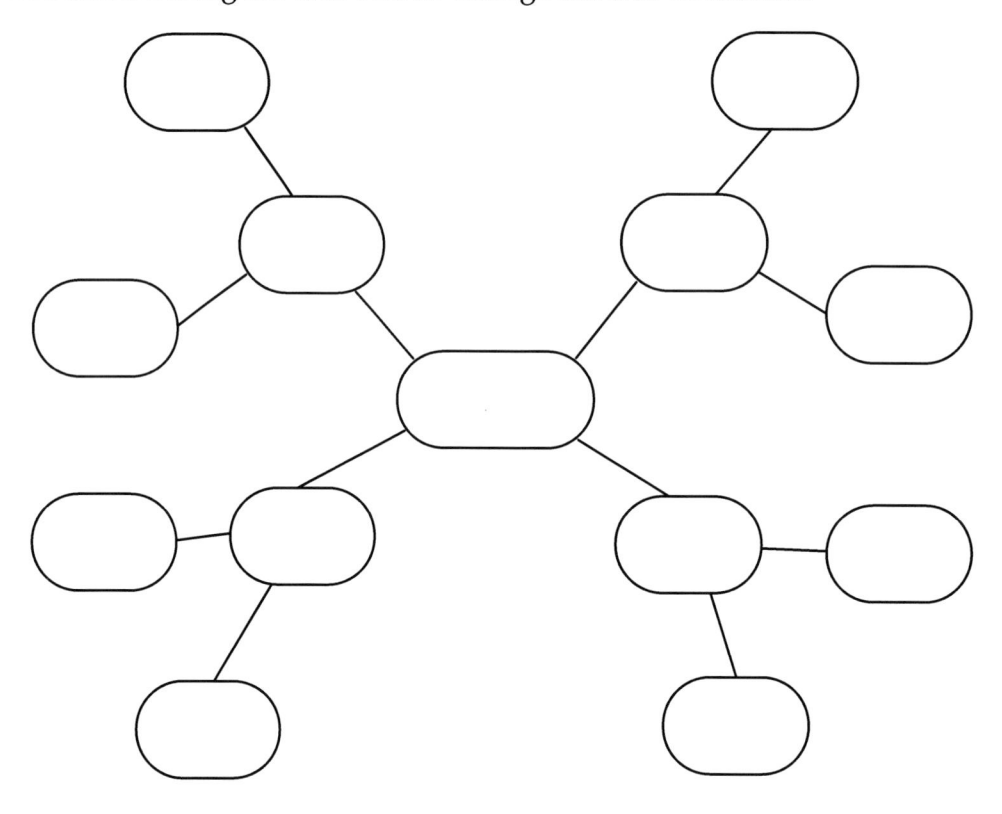

Narrow Your Topic

Now analyze your web. Then write your narrowed topic.

_____

Define Your Purpose

What do you want to show about your topic? Write a thesis statement that shows your purpose.

_____

_____

Identify Your Audience

Write who your audience is and how this affects your writing.

_____

_____

Cause and Effect *(continued)*

Drafting   Use one of the following graphic organizers to help keep track of what you want to include in your essay.

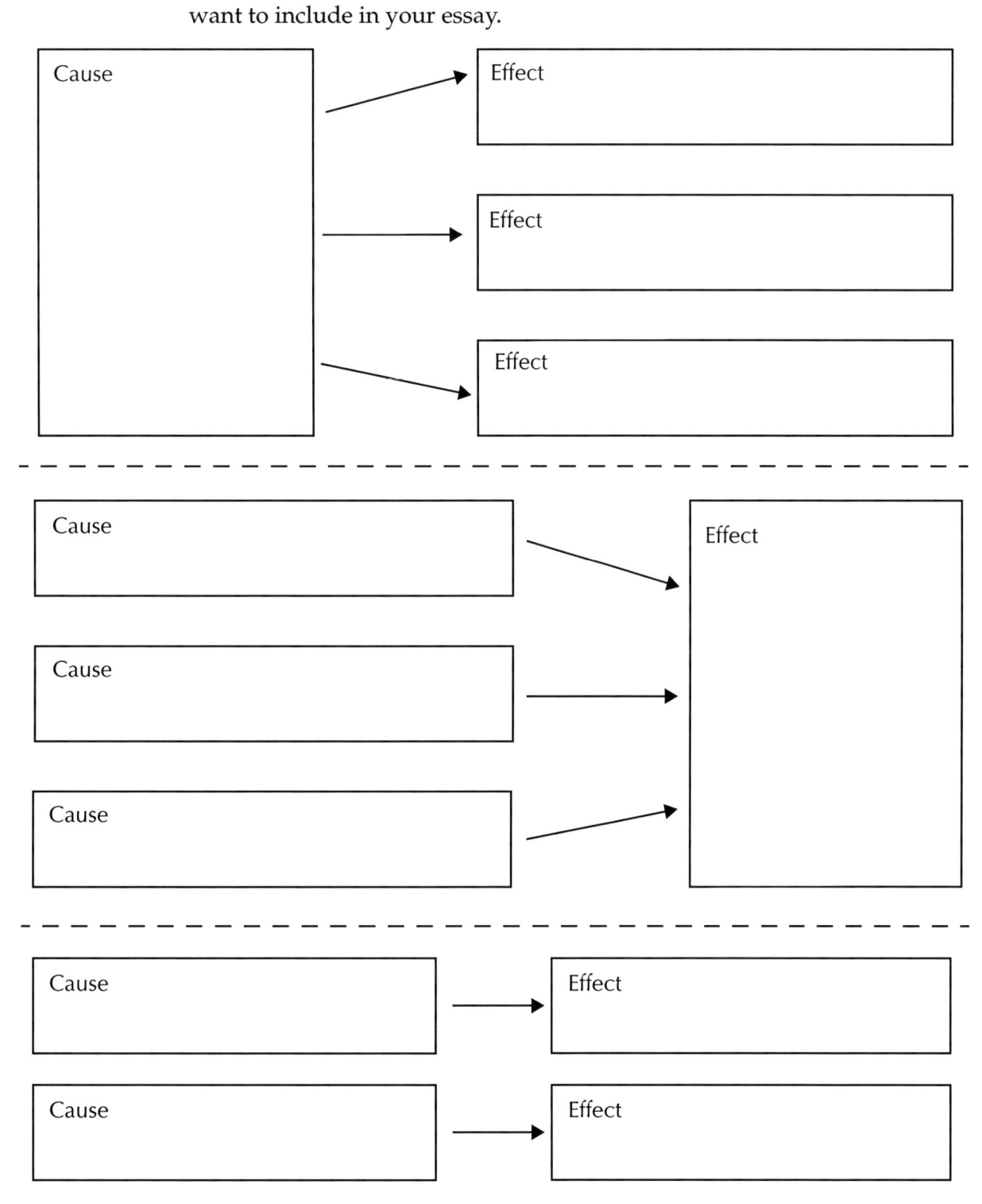

Cause	→	Effect
	→	Effect
	→	Effect

Cause	→	Effect
Cause	→	
Cause	→	

Cause	→	Effect
Cause	→	Effect

Now write your first draft on a separate sheet of paper.

Cause and Effect *(continued)*

Revising and Publishing

Revising

Reread your first draft, looking for places where your ideas and organization can be improved. Some questions you may want to ask yourself about your cause-and-effect essay include:

- Is my thesis statement clear?
- Are the causes and effects true?
- Are the cause-and-effect relationships clear?
- Have I used cause-and-effect words?

Peer Editing

You may want to ask a peer to be a sounding board and to comment on your essay. Your revising checklist from your teacher can also help by giving you general guidelines to follow. Now you can write your second draft.

Proofreading

After you have made your idea and organization revisions in your second draft, it is time to concentrate on the mechanics. Check for grammatical, spelling, and punctuation errors. Refer to your proofreading checklist from your teacher.

Publishing

After you have polished your essay, publish it in a form acceptable to your teacher. Be sure your final draft is clean, clear, and easy to read. Create a title that captures the reader.

Lesson 11
Chronological Order

From the moment we open our eyes in the morning, we begin thinking in chronological order: *Okay, I have to get myself out of this very comfortable bed; then I have to put some food in my system; next I need to shower and put on some clothes; finally, I have to gather all my stuff and make it out to the bus.* Note how logical this stream of thought is. You think about putting on clothes AFTER you shower; you think of gathering all your stuff BEFORE you head out to the bus stop. Also, note how effective this thinking is—you have an objective, which is to make it to the bus stop on time. Everything that you do—getting out of bed, eating breakfast, showering, dressing, gathering your stuff—brings you closer to meeting this objective.

Chrono or *chron* is derived from the Greek *khronos*, which means "time." Essays written using chronological order arrange events as they happen in time with the purpose of attaining a specific objective. Chronological-order essays have one of two purposes: to recount events, incidents, or occurrences as they happened in time, or to explain how to do something. Chronological-order essays often shed light on cause-and-effect relationships as one event in time or one step in a process naturally leads to a specific outcome.

Model

If you are writing to explain the evolution of the Internet, your thesis statement will focus on the earliest use of the Internet and then allude to what the Internet is used for today. You might begin with the following thesis statement:

> What began as a highly specialized and secret means of continuing military communication in the case of nuclear disaster has become a virtual coffeehouse open for business around the world.

The body of the essay would recount the events that brought the Internet out from behind the curtain of military secrecy and into the homes, schools, and businesses of people everywhere.

Similarly, if you are writing to explain the steps involved in changing a tire, your thesis statement would be very general. The body paragraphs would go on to explain each step to reach the desired outcome.

Chronological Order *(continued)*

Changing a tire is not glamorous, but these six steps go far toward ensuring safety on the road. With the proper equipment and preparation, you can rely on yourself to change a flat.

First, always keep an inflated spare tire in your car. Without this vital piece of equipment, you cannot continue.

Once you have the spare out, find your jack and your lug wrench. Many jacks have a special holder somewhere on the car; you should know where it is. If you don't, your owner's manual will tell you.

Use the lug wrench to loosen the lug nuts. These are the metal nuts that hold the wheel on. You should loosen them in a star pattern. First loosen a nut near the top of the circle of nuts. Then loosen one roughly opposite it. Then return to a nut next to the first. Continue until you have loosened all the nuts.

Next, attach the jack to the car following the safety instructions on the jack. Lift the car so that the tire just clears the road.

Remove the loosened lug nuts. Be sure to put the nuts in a safe container. Take the flat tire off the vehicle.

Next, fit the spare tire onto the car. Put the lug nuts on loosely. Then tighten them, following a star pattern as you did when you removed them.

After the tire is firmly attached, you can lower the car and remove the jack. You have changed a flat tire!

Finally, when you arrive at your destination, be sure to have the flat tire repaired, or replace it. If your spare is a mini tire to be used only temporarily, you will have to put a full-size tire back on. To do this, follow the steps above!

Good Writing Tip: Use Chronological Order Words

Strong chronological-order essays feature words that provide a clear and logical sequence of events for readers. Some such words are

Chronological Order Words	
after	meanwhile
at the same time	next
before	preceding
concurrently	presently
currently	previously
during	shortly thereafter
finally	simultaneously
first, second, third, and so on	subsequently
followed by	then

Chronological Order (continued)

Try It Read the following chronological-order passage. Then answer the questions that follow.

Henry's Wives

Born in 1491 in England, Henry VIII succeeded his father, Henry VII, in 1509. He was thought to have had a "golden youth," one during which the charms of the handsome and athletic Henry worked their magic. A strange turn of events occurred when Henry VIII ascended to the throne, however. Becoming king marked the physical and social decline of Henry VIII. Henry's legacy tells the tale of a voracious eater who broke up the Roman Catholic Church and went through six wives in a fevered attempt to father a male heir.

Henry VIII's first wife also happened to be his brother's widow, Katharine of Aragon. The two were married in 1509 and remained so until Henry divorced Katharine in 1529 for her inability to bear him a male heir. Henry claimed that Katharine was too old to give him a son. Henry's relationship with Katharine produced one child, Mary I, but the most notable outcome of this marriage is the rift it caused in the Roman Catholic Church. Refused a divorce by the pope, Henry appointed himself head of the Christian Church of England. Henry then granted himself a divorce and swiftly moved on to wife number two.

A member of the highly respected Howard family, Anne Boleyn became Queen of England in 1533. She and Henry brought Elizabeth I into the world; however, a daughter was not what Henry desired. To hasten his quest for a mate who could mother a male heir, Henry accused Anne of being unfaithful, and in 1536 Anne Boleyn was beheaded for her alleged infidelity. Days after Anne's execution, Henry married Jane Seymour, who had been a lady-in-waiting to both Katharine of Aragon and Anne Boleyn. This third marriage brought Edward VI into the world, much to the elation of the King. Jane Seymour died shortly after giving life to her husband's heir, who died of tuberculosis in 1553.

Henry's fourth marriage was his shortest. Henry married Anne of Cleves in January of 1540 and divorced her in July of that same year, making room for Catherine Howard, whom Henry wed in the latter months of 1540. Catherine Howard met with the same horrific fate as Anne Boleyn. In 1542 she was beheaded for alleged infidelity. The execution of Howard allowed Henry to marry his sixth and final wife, Catherine Parr. She did not provide Henry with any heirs, male or female, but she did manage to survive her husband, who died in 1547.

1. What is the thesis statement of this passage?

2. List the chronology words that show the order in which events happened.

Chronological Order *(continued)*

Application Read the list of topics below. Then read the provided selections. After you have finished reading, write a chronological-order essay based on one of the topics.

Topics

1. On March 15, 44 B.C., a day known as the Ides of March, the Roman general and powerful leader Julius Caesar was assassinated. Caesar had ample warning of his impending death, however. Read through the following diary, journal, and household record entries, letters, and miscellaneous papers written by those closest to Caesar. In a well-organized essay, enumerate all the warnings Caesar received, in the order that he received them. The objective of your essay is to show your reader how easily Caesar could have saved his own life had he just listened to those who cared about his well-being.

2. The conspiracy to assassinate Julius Caesar grew out of one man's jealousy of Caesar's power and position in the Roman Empire. This man was Caius Cassius. Read through the following diary, journal, and household record entries, letters, and miscellaneous papers written by those closest to Caesar. In a well-organized essay, enumerate all the hints of Cassius' danger in the order that they occur. The objective of your essay is to show your reader how easily Caesar could have saved his own life had he just followed his own instincts with regard to Cassius' character.

3. Caesar is thought to have been a very superstitious man; however, Caesar only believed superstitions when they benefited him. In other words, if someone predicted something bad about Caesar, Caesar would ignore the prediction. Similarly, if something strange and extraordinary happened but the event did not bolster Caesar's confidence in his future, then Caesar would simply ignore the event. Read the following diary, journal, and household record entries, letters, and miscellaneous papers written by those closest to Caesar. In a well-organized essay, enumerate all the superstition-inspired warnings and strange events, in the order in which they occur, that, if taken into consideration, could have saved Caesar's life. The objective of your essay is to show your reader how easily Caesar could have saved his own life had he placed importance on all the strange happenings that occurred in the months and days leading up to the Ides of March.

Chronological Order *(continued)*

If Only Caesar Had Heeded Their Warnings

The following is a fictional adaptation of the actual events leading up to Caesar's assassination as presented in Plutarch's *Lives of Illustrious Men* and William Shakespeare's tragedy *Julius Caesar*.

From the diary of Calpurnia, Caesar's wife:

December 10, 45 B.C.

Something rather strange occurred today as the mighty Caesar and I awaited the start of the footrace at the Feast of Lupercal, a celebration of fertility. Marcus Antony, who was running in the race, approached us; Caesar asked Antony to place his hands upon me in the hope of enhancing my ability to provide Caesar with a male heir; and as Antony moved away from us, a soothsayer, one who speaks of truths yet unknown to the general public, cried from the throngs of people, "Caesar! Beware the Ides of March!" Caesar asked his senators to set this man before him, which his obedient senators did. As the aged soothsayer was brought before the powerful Caesar, again he said, "Caesar! Beware the Ides of March!" Caesar reacted with annoyance, calling the soothsayer a dreamer and pushing him aside.

I know my Caesar is wise and honorable; I should trust in his presumption that this soothsayer speaks of nothing but nonsense, but I like it not!

December 20, 45 B.C.

Caesar commented to Antony that he thinks Cassius has a "lean and hungry look"; Caesar thinks such men are dangerous. Antony told Caesar not to worry about Cassius. I hope Antony knows what he is talking about. I hear the soothsayer's words echoing in my mind at every moment. I'm quite uneasy, but my dear Caesar tells me not to worry, that all is well. For the sake of all, I hope Caesar is right.

March 14, 44 B.C.

11:58 P.M. I've had the most terrible dream! Blood was spouting from hundreds of holes in the statue of Caesar that stands outside the senate house in the center of Rome and lusty Romans were bathing their hands in Caesar's blood with menacing, evil smiles on their faces. I swear that one of the Romans was that sneaky Caius Cassius, but it is difficult for me to remember exactly who the men were. They screamed, "Liberty! Freedom! Enfranchisement! Tyranny is dead!" and sneered at the bloody statue of Caesar. What does this mean?! I must speak of my fears to Caesar immediately! The Roman senators plan to crown him King of Rome tomorrow on the steps of the senate house, and I do fear for his life.

(continued)

Chronological Order *(continued)*

If Only Caesar Had Heeded Their Warnings (continued)

March 15, 44 B.C.

4:45 A.M. I've told Caesar of my dream. I also informed him of the other unimaginable horrors I dreamed of last night—ghosts did soar above the senate house, a lion gave birth upon the steps of the senate, the skies did battle and roared thunderously, and the clouds did rain blood upon Caesar's statue! This is a terrible time! I've begged Caesar not to go to the senate this morning. He is reluctant to stay at home, but I do think he will listen to me; after all, he loves me and does not like to see me so upset. I must return to Caesar, to ensure that he stays at home today. Oh my! I've just realized something! Today is the Ides of March! I must to Caesar go!

*****

From the household records kept by Caesar's servants:

Late in the evening on the eve of the Ides of March: As I was walking about this evening, I saw Caius Cassius speaking with Marcus Brutus, Casca, and other Roman senators outside Marcus Brutus' home. They were all wearing hoods over their heads, so it was hard to tell for sure who was who, but I am positive I saw that sneaky Cassius pretending to stab an invisible victim. The men around him seemed to be energized by Cassius' exaggerated stabbing motion. To make this night even more strange, when I returned to Caesar's household, her Ladyship Calpurnia did cry out in her sleep, "Help! They do slay Caesar!" The heavens are alive with terrible winds, and comets fly through the night sky: Such nights occur only when something horrible is about to happen.

Early in the morning on the Ides of March: Caesar ordered me to sacrifice a beast to the almighty gods to see if today, the day on which Caesar is to be crowned King of Rome, is a favorable day for such a significant and triumphant event. There was no heart inside the beast, a very bad omen. Caesar seems unmoved by this unfavorable happening, though; I think he means to go forth with the day's proceedings, despite Calpurnia's and the gods' warnings.

8:45 A.M. on the Ides of March: Decius Brutus, Marcus Brutus, Caius Cassius, Casca, and four more Romans have come to escort Caesar to the senate. Calpurnia is begging Caesar to stay at home with her, but Caesar does not want to appear fearful and weak in front of these powerful Romans, so he has agreed to go forth to the senate house, and is preparing to leave as I write this . . . Cassius, oddly enough, is assuring Calpurnia that everything will be well, that she need not worry about the safety of her husband.

(continued)

*****

Chronological Order *(continued)*

If Only Caesar Had Heeded Their Warnings (continued)

A letter written by Artemidorus, friend of Caesar, teacher of logic and writing, at eight o'clock in the morning of the Ides of March:

Caesar, beware of Brutus; take heed of Cassius; come not near Casca; have an eye to Cinna; trust not Trebonius; mark well Entellus Cimber; Decius Brutus loves thee not; thou hast wronged Caius Ligarius. There is but one mind in all these men, and it is bent against Caesar. If you beest not immortal, look about you; security gives way to conspiracy. The mighty gods defend thee!

Thy friend, Artemidorus

As Caesar walks the street to the senate house at 8:55 A.M., Artemidorus attempts to give Caesar this letter, saying, "If you take the time to read this letter, dear Caesar, you may live! If you ignore me, your fate is to die!" Caesar refuses to take the letter.

*****

From papers found in the home of a Roman commoner:

March 15, 44 B.C.

It is 20 minutes past nine in the morning and I have just witnessed the most terrible event! As Caesar walked the streets to the senate house, where the people did mean to crown him king, Caesar reproached a soothsayer who stood amongst the crowds of people. Caesar said to the soothsayer, rather sarcastically, "Soothsayer! I see the Ides of March have come! What think you of your foolish warning!?" The soothsayer lowered his eyes from those of the mighty Caesar and said quietly, "Ay, the Ides of March have come, Caesar, but they have not yet gone." I did not think much of this exchange, until Caesar entered the senate house. Mere minutes after the great doors of the senate were closed, Cassius opened them and with bloody hands gesticulating, he screamed, "Liberty! Freedom! Enfranchisement! Tyranny is dead! The man who would be a tyrant and turn us all into slaves has been slain! Rejoice! Caesar is dead!"

Today, March 15, 44 B.C., at nine in the morning, Julius Caesar was stabbed to death by the very men who honored him.

Chronological Order *(continued)*

Prewriting

Brainstorming

Brainstorm ideas about your topic. Change the web as needed.

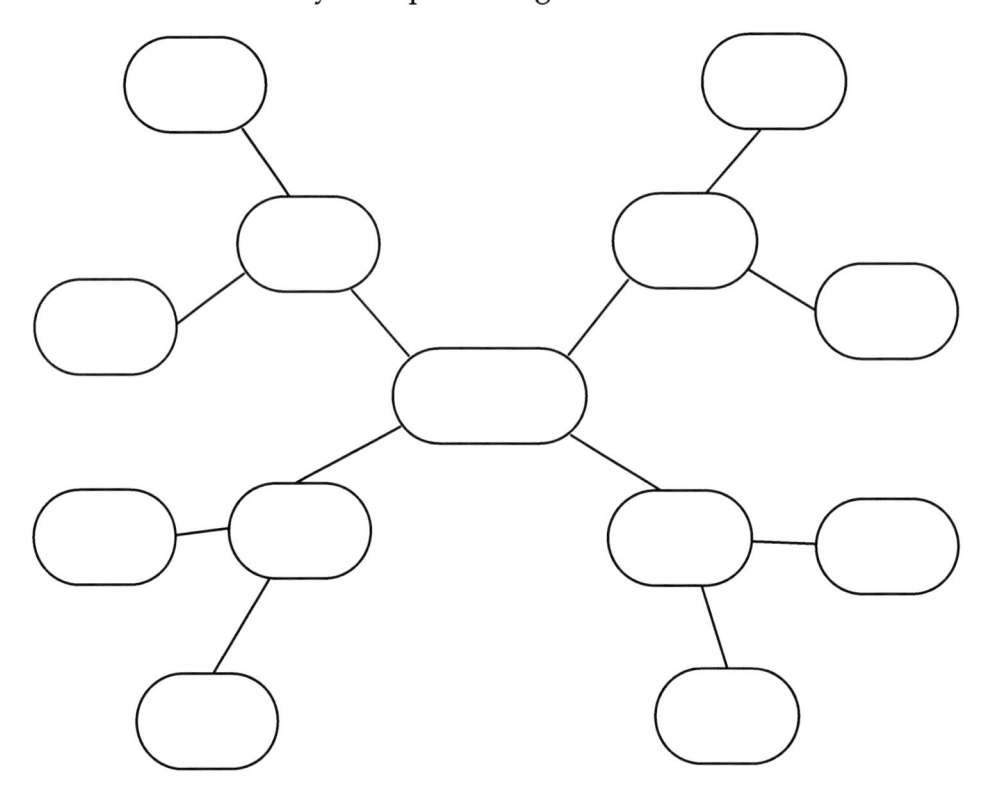

Narrow Your Topic

Now analyze your web. Then write your narrowed topic.

_____

Define Your Purpose

What do you want to show about your topic? Write your purpose in a thesis statement.

_____

_____

Identify Your Audience

Write who your audience is and how this affects your writing.

_____

_____

Chronological Order *(continued)*

Drafting Use the graphic organizer below to write the first draft of your chronological-order essay. Pay particular attention to the order of events.

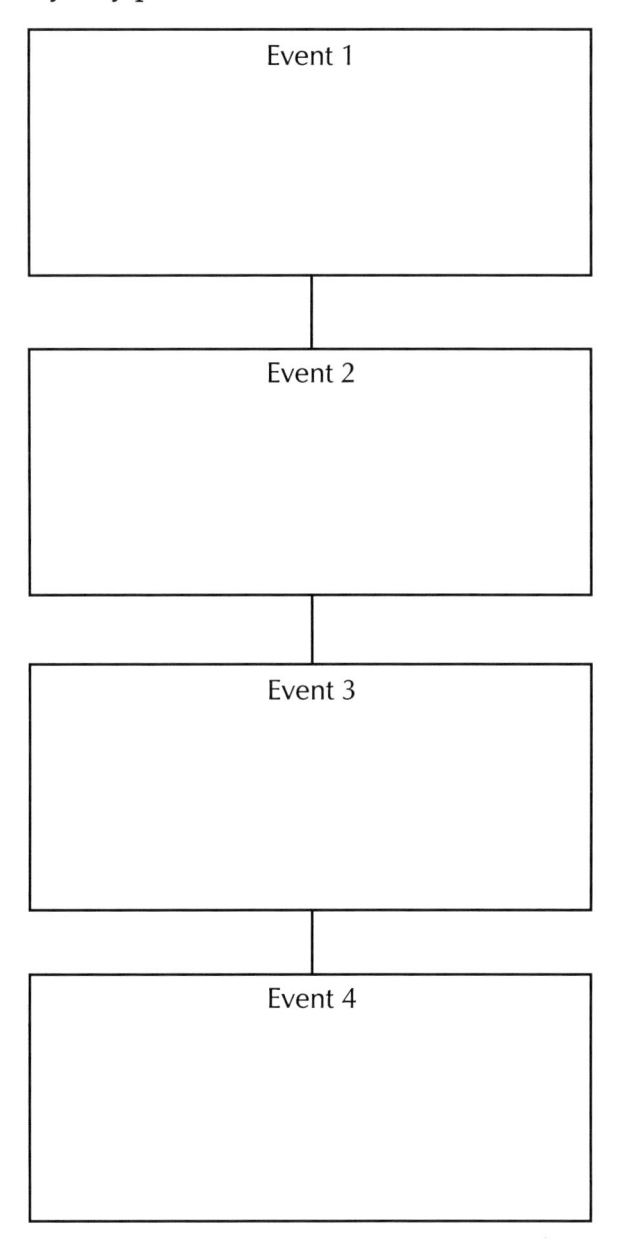

```
┌─────────────────────────┐
│        Event 1          │
│                         │
└─────────────────────────┘
            │
┌─────────────────────────┐
│        Event 2          │
│                         │
└─────────────────────────┘
            │
┌─────────────────────────┐
│        Event 3          │
│                         │
└─────────────────────────┘
            │
┌─────────────────────────┐
│        Event 4          │
│                         │
└─────────────────────────┘
```

Now write the first draft of your essay.

Chronological Order *(continued)*

Revising and Publishing

Revising

Reread your first draft, looking for places where your ideas and organization can be improved. Some questions you may want to ask yourself about your chronological-order essay include the following:

- Is my thesis statement clear?
- Is the order of events clear?
- Have I used chronological-order words?

Peer Editing

You may want to ask a peer to be a sounding board and to comment on your essay. Your revising checklist from your teacher can also help by giving you general guidelines to follow. Now you can write your second draft.

Proofreading

After you have made your idea and organization revisions in your second draft, it is time to concentrate on the mechanics. Check for grammatical, spelling, and punctuation errors. Refer to your proofreading checklist from your teacher.

Publishing

After you have polished your essay, publish it in a form acceptable to your teacher. Be sure your essay is clean, clear, and easy to read. Create an interesting title.

Part 3
Practice Readings

Practice Reading A

Female Athletes and Injury

Since the inception in 1972 of Title IX, a law requiring colleges and universities to expend a proportionate amount of funds for both male and female athletics, females and sports have been getting to know one another better. According to an article in *WIN News*, the number of women who participate in high school sports is up from one in twenty-seven in 1970 to one in three in 1997. This is an amazing increase, and one that is of great importance to the world of sports. There has been another increase, however, one that is not worthy of celebration: injuries among female athletes.

An injury that has reached disconcerting proportions in female athletes aged 15–25 is the dreaded torn anterior cruciate ligament (ACL), an injury that sidelines 30,000 female athletes each year. The ACL connects the thighbone to the shinbone; it is like a bridge that closes the gap between the top part of the leg and the bottom part of the leg. When it is torn, there is a "pop," a flash of excruciating pain, swelling, and immediate immobility.

The Women's National Basketball Association (WNBA) has dubbed ACL injuries an epidemic that is decimating their league. And basketball is not the only sport denied elite female athletes due to this debilitating injury; soccer has its share of players who are rendered unable to play because of torn ACLs. Take Brandi Chastain, the American soccer player who scored the winning goal in the World Cup final; she has had the great misfortune of tearing both ACLs. Chastain's story differs from the majority of women who suffer ACL injuries, because Chastain was able to fight her way back into competition not once, but twice. Most female athletes who tear ACLs are not so resilient and are forced to give up the sports they love.

Why is it that female athletes are 80 percent more likely than their male counterparts to suffer an ACL tear? The answer is obvious: Women are built differently from men, and these differences in physiology are the cause of female susceptibility to torn ACLs.

It is no secret that women's hips are generally wider than men's. This causes the femur—the thighbone—and the quadriceps—the major muscle at the front of the thigh—to angle inward to the knee much more sharply in women than in men. These sharp angles stress the knee ligaments. Also, the actual anterior cruciate ligament anchors itself to the lower part of the leg through a notch at the end of the femur. This notch is much narrower in women than it is in men. This narrowness inhibits the range of motion of the ligament, again causing stress at the knee. Lastly, women's leg muscles develop differently than

(continued)

Practice Reading A (continued)

Female Athletes and Injury (continued)

men's. While men's quadriceps and hamstrings—muscles that line the front and back of the thigh, respectively—develop evenly, women tend to have much stronger quad muscles than hamstring muscles. This imbalance in muscle strength places an inordinate amount of stress at the front of the knee, just behind the kneecap, which eventually leads to a torn ACL.

Oh, the irony. Since the beginning of time, women have been fighting for equality with men. Now that equality in the arena of athletics is on the horizon, women are discovering that "equal" may not be exactly what they have been striving for. For generations, female athletes have been trained in the same manner as male athletes. Now that it is known that for every man who suffers an ACL injury there are six women who are downed with ACL injuries, coaches and trainers throughout the United States have begun to address the ACL problem by creating strength training programs specifically targeting the female athlete.

Because the bulk of ACL injuries occur when athletes are landing and pivoting, trainers have honed in on female biomechanics, which refers to how women run and stop, jump and land. Female athletes are trained to keep their knees bent when decelerating, pivoting, and landing jumps. It is critical, however, that the bent knee does not jut out over the athlete's toes; rather, the knee should be directly in line with the big toe. Athletes work out on trampolines, pogo sticks, and skateboards to perfect this key positioning. Balancing on one leg while catching a ball is another tactic trainers use to better female biomechanics. Stretching and strength training, with a focus on the hamstrings, are also popular in female training programs. The results of these training programs, sometimes called jump training, are promising. Not only are female athletes better able to maintain healthy biomechanics after completing these specially designed programs, but they are also stronger, and most importantly, female athletes have a newfound awareness of their bodies and of what they need to do to protect their knees.

Practice Reading B

It Can Only Be Love

If you have a pet, then you know that animals and humans share a very special bond. For pet owners, the nature of this bond is quite clear: Love, compassion, and trust are its primary components. For scientists, however, this bond is much more difficult to explain. There is no tried and true way to gather data that proves that animals experience, understand, and respond to human emotion. Despite this lack of hard evidence, the soft data is overwhelming and very convincing.

Clara is a Chicago, Illinois, tabby cat whose unusual behavior saved her owners. Clara's "mom" and "dad" were sleeping soundly early one morning when a sudden noise awoke Clara's "dad." He opened his eyes to see a shadowy figure looking into the bedroom from the fire escape outside the window. Clara, somehow aware of an intrusion, charged from her bed in the living room into the bedroom, her fur puffed out, her teeth bared, and her claws drawn. She was growling like an attack dog and threw herself repeatedly against the window screen. Clara scared off the intruder and, although science will not recognize Clara's actions as emotionally motivated, it is hard to ignore the tabby cat's intense anger at the intruder. No one was going to harm Clara's "mom" and "dad" if she had anything to do with it. Clara's owners were grateful for their pet tabby's loyalty and devotion to her family, which *they* assumed prompted her into action.

Scientifically speaking, Clara's behavior can be attributed to altruism, which is an animal's tendency to assist others like them. Charles Darwin, renowned naturalist, proposed that altruism has nothing to do with emotion and everything to do with survival. Apparently, if a species provides assistance to others of the same species, then that species has a much better chance of survival. If you have ever seen chimpanzees or other primates grooming one another, you may have thought, "Oh, isn't that sweet. They're taking care of one another." Darwin would laugh scornfully at this presumption. To Darwin, primate-on-primate grooming is a perfect example of altruism. Grooming is a selfish act that promotes the health and longevity of the species, for if one chimp grooms parasites off the back of another chimp, then that chimp will return the favor, and a pack of healthy primates will continue reproducing their species. Perhaps what was perceived as bravery, courage, and devotion by Clara's owners can be written off as an act of altruism, a self-preserving, unemotional response to danger. Still, how can science explain the story of Robe?

Robe, a German shepherd-collie mix, somehow knew that his owner needed

(continued)

Practice Reading B (continued)

It Can Only Be Love (continued)

help. One icy New England evening, Robe's owner left his comfortable and warm home to walk across the street to choir practice. Because the night was so cold, wet, and miserable, Robe remained inside with the rest of the family instead of accompanying his "dad." A few minutes after "dad" left the house, Robe became agitated and began pacing back and forth in front of the door leading outside. Thinking Robe needed to use the doggie outhouse, Robe's "mom" let him out. Moments later, the family heard shuffling and struggling at the back door. Upon opening the back door, Robe's family discovered that their dad had fallen and severely broken his ankle and had been accompanied home by who else but Robe. What prompted Robe into action on that seemingly typical winter evening? Why would Robe leave the comfy coziness of his home to help his owner if not for love? Does Darwin's altruism explain Robe's response? No. To show further the depth of the love, care, and compassion that Robe exhibited toward his owner, it is important to report what happened when Robe's "dad" returned from the emergency room later that same evening. The family gathered around their father who was resting in a chair with his right leg, which was enveloped by a heavy cast, elevated. Robe maneuvered himself right up close to where his "dad" was resting and placed his head ever so gently atop the cast.

Until very recently, all evidence of animals' emotions has been anecdotal, based on unofficial stories, or empirical, based on isolated experiences, like the preceeding ones. Neither of these evidence-gathering methods is accepted as scientific method and, therefore, all such data is considered invalid by the scientific world. Further, scientists are very wary of anthropomorphizing animals. Anthropomorphism is the practice of assigning human qualities and emotion to nonhumans. Pet owners do this all the time. In fact, part of the joy of having pets is bestowing upon them all the emotions and feelings that humans experience every day, such as boredom, hunger, fear, embarrassment, anger, and impatience. Scientists, however, think that it is careless of humans to assume that what humans experience can be experienced in a similar way by animals. But how else can Rover's unbridled happiness at his owner's arrival home from work be explained? What is the cause of Fluffy's hasty retreat behind the couch after misreading her leap from the windowsill to the top of the bookcase if not embarrassment? Surely, animals experience emotions that are comparable to those of humans.

Recent data proves that the brains of humans and the brains of animals are more similar than science had believed. Laura Tangley, author of "Animal Emotions," which appeared in *U.S. News & World Report*, states that "[s]cientists who study the biology of emotions, a field still in its infancy, are discovering many similarities between the brains of humans and other animals . . . . emotions seem to arise from ancient parts of the brain" in both humans and animals.

(continued)

Practice Reading B (continued)

It Can Only Be Love (continued)

Compounding the similarities between the human brain and the animal brain is the study of brain chemistry. Scientists have discovered that animals and humans both possess dopamine, which is a pleasure-inducing chemical in the brain. When rats were given a delicacy of cheese to eat, the amount of dopamine in their brains increased, which is exactly what happens to humans when given favorite foods to ingest. Also, Magnetic Resonance Imaging (MRI), which is an advanced way of taking very detailed pictures of various organs, has shown that animals' brains react in the same ways as humans' when in similar emotional states.

Advancements in technology have led to advancements in humans' willingness to accept that animals just may understand more about our lives than previously thought. Additionally, it seems as though science is catching up to what pet owners and animal lovers have believed all along: That special bond between humans and their pets is fueled by the true-blue emotion of love.

Practice Reading C

Sandra Cisneros: Author Who Tells the Stories of Strong Hispanic Women

Sandra Cisneros is a new voice in American literature. Some think she is our best Mexican-American woman writer. She writes stories that have never been told, filling the void of stories about Hispanic-American women.

Cisneros was born in 1954 in Chicago, Illinois. Her father was Mexican; her mother, Mexican American. Cisneros had six brothers. She has said that she felt as if she grew up with seven fathers telling her what to do.

In her early years, Sandra and her family moved many times. When her father became homesick for Mexico, they would go back to Mexico City. They always returned to Chicago, but to a different street, a different apartment, and a different school. But all the neighborhoods they tried had one thing in common: They were poor.

All this moving was hard on Cisneros. She became very shy. She had few friends, and she spent a lot of time by herself. Cisneros developed a strong love of reading during this time. Later, Cisneros said that her aloneness "was good for a would-be writer. It allowed . . . time to think . . . to imagine . . . to read and prepare." Cisneros became an observer of other people. She watched and remembered how they looked, how they talked, and what they did.

Cisneros's parents had little education, but they stressed education to their children. Her father worked as a carpenter, but he wanted more for his children. He often told them to learn to use their heads, not their hands. When Cisneros wanted to go to college, her father agreed. He thought that college would be a good place for her to find a husband. Cisneros had other ideas. At Loyola University, she majored in English. She wanted to become a writer.

Cisneros started by writing poems. She studied for her master's degree at the University of Iowa Writer's Workshop. She soon found out that she had little in common with the other students. She felt out of place, almost foreign. Later she described herself as a "yellow weed among the city's cracks." Her classmates had been bred as "hothouse flowers."

One day in class, students were telling about the houses where they had grown up. As she listened, Cisneros realized she had no such house in her memories. Cisneros suddenly knew why she felt different from the other students: She *was* different. Her race and her culture were completely different; she was a Mexican woman. At that moment, she accepted herself for who she was. She realized that her voice was unique. She would write about things her classmates could never write about.

(continued)

Practice Reading C (continued)

Sandra Cisneros: Author Who Tells the Stories of Strong Hispanic Women (continued)

From this awakening, her first book was born. *The House on Mango Street* is the story of Esperanza, a young girl growing up in a poor Hispanic neighborhood in Chicago. Through her eyes, the reader sees the lives of the people living there. In the course of the book, Esperanza learns to understand both herself and her culture. By the end of the book, Esperanza has decided how she will escape her poverty: through her writing. But at the close of the book, she is reminded that leaving Mango Street does not mean leaving who she is. In fact, the story of Esperanza is the story of Cisneros herself.

With the publication of *The House on Mango Street* in 1984, Cisneros became recognized as a major new talent. Today the book is being used in schools and colleges across the country. After finishing *The House on Mango Street*, Cisneros received a one-year National Endowment for the Arts fellowship. She moved to Texas where she wrote a book of poetry, *My Wicked, Wicked Ways*. This book got great reviews. Yet Cisneros was unable to make a living from her writing. She worked at odd jobs, trying to make ends meet. This time was the low point of her life.

Finally, she was offered a teaching job in California. Later, she was awarded another NEA fellowship. She was back on her feet.

Meanwhile, in New York City, a literary agent had read *The House on Mango Street*. She wanted to help Ciseros publish more books. It took nearly four years, but finally the two women got together. This led to the publication, in 1991, of Cisneros's third book, *Women Hollering Creek and Other Stories*. The title story has been called one of the great short stories in American literature. All her characters are strong women. They are women of different ages, different races, and different situations telling their stories.

Today Cisneros lives in San Antonio, Texas. She continues to write, and her fourth book, *Loose Women*, was published in 1994.

Cisneros hopes to give something back to the Hispanic community. While she has left her childhood of poverty behind, it is still a part of her. As one of her characters in *The House on Mango Street* tells Esperanza:

You will always be Esperanza. You will always be Mango Street. You can't erase what you know. You can't forget who you are. You must remember to come back. For the ones who cannot leave as easily as you.

Cisneros will never leave the Hispanic community. She is herself a symbol of the Mexican woman. And through her writing, her story is being heard at last.

Practice Reading D

Antonia Hernandez: Civil Rights Lawyer

The Mexican-American Legal Defense Fund (MALDEF) is a Hispanic civil rights group. Antonia Hernandez is MALDEF's president and general counsel. MALDEF was founded in 1968. Its purpose is to protect the legal rights of Mexican Americans.

MALDEF works for better education for Mexican Americans. The group also seeks job training for minorities. Since 1985, Antonia Hernandez has led MALDEF. She has fought for the rights of Hispanics and other minority groups. "We are the Hispanic community's law firm," she says.

Antonia Hernandez was born in 1948 in Torreon, Mexico. When she was eight, her family moved to East Los Angeles. Her father was a gardener. Her mother stayed home to raise the six Hernandez children. The Hernandez family was poor, but it was strong and loving. Hernandez's parents encouraged their children to do well in school. They also gave the children a strong belief in helping others.

Hernandez trained to be a teacher. She graduated from UCLA in 1973 with a teaching certificate. She began working in a ghetto program for teenagers. Soon she decided that she could help kids more by doing something about the unfair laws that were keeping them back. So Hernandez went to UCLA law school After graduation, she became a legal aid lawyer. Legal aid lawyers provide legal help for the poor. She also fought for pro-minority bills in the state legislature.

In 1977, she married Michael Stern, who was also a lawyer. The couple later had three children.

In 1978, Hernandez was offered a new job. She would work for the Senate Judiciary Committee under Senator Ted Kennedy. She turned down the job. She was happy doing legal aid work to help the poor of Los Angeles. And she didn't really want to leave her hometown. The committee couldn't believe that she had turned down the job because she loved her legal aid work. They thought the real reason must be the salary. So they offered her more money. Hernandez turned down the job again. But her husband finally talked her into it. He told her it was a career move that was too good to pass up. So Hernandez moved to Washington, D.C., to work for the Judiciary Committee. She advised the committee on immigration and human rights issues.

Hernandez worked for the committee for two years. But, in 1980, the Democrats lost control of the Senate. That meant that the Republicans would take over the Judiciary Committee. Antonia Hernandez was out of a job.

(continued)

Antonia Hernandez: Civil Rights Lawyer (continued)

The next day she had a job offer from MALDEF. She joined its Washington, D.C., office. She quickly worked her way up through the ranks. By 1981, she was heading the office. While working with MALDEF, Hernandez has been able to get many laws passed to help Hispanic Americans. She has fought for fair funding for public schools. She has gone to court to make sure school district lines were drawn fairly. She has also worked for more jobs for Hispanic Americans. Hernandez fought against a bill that would have required Hispanics to carry I.D. cards. She said this would lead to discrimination. The defeat of this bill was one of her proudest achievements.

Hernandez has worked hard for bilingual education. "Bilingual" means being able to speak two languages equally well. Many Hispanic Americans speak Spanish as their first language. Later they learn English. Hernandez herself had a difficult experience as a child. When she started school, she spoke only Spanish. She was placed in a class with a teacher who spoke only English. She had to "sink or swim." It was hard until she finally learned enough English to get by. Consequently, Hernandez believes in bilingual education. The idea is to teach children in their native language first. They learn English on the side. Later they go on to regular classes taught only in English. At the same time, they continue to learn to read and write Spanish. This way they learn both languages well.

Bilingual education is controversial. It is a costly program. And some say it doesn't work any better than just putting children into regular classrooms. On the other hand, some say Spanish-speaking children should not have to give up their native language and culture.

Living in Washington, D.C., has made Hernandez more aware of the different groups of Hispanic Americans. In Los Angeles, where she grew up, most Hispanic Americans are Mexican. On the East Coast, she has met Puerto Ricans, Cubans, and South and Central Americans. This has given her a broader view of Hispanic Americans and their needs. Hernandez has worked for unity among civil rights groups. She worked with the NAACP, the largest African-American civil rights group, on the 1992 Civil Rights Bill. She believes that all minority groups should work together for a stronger America.

In a July 8, 1991, issue of *Time* magazine, she is quoted as stating, "By acknowledging the contributions made to our country by Native Americans and by Hispanics and blacks and Asians, we're really strengthening our unity." Hernandez feels that all these groups have made vital contributions to what our country is today. And all these groups should be treated fairly and have equal rights.

PART 4
Graphic Organizers

BRAINSTORMING WEB

Use this chart to brainstorm writing ideas. Add or subtract circles as needed.

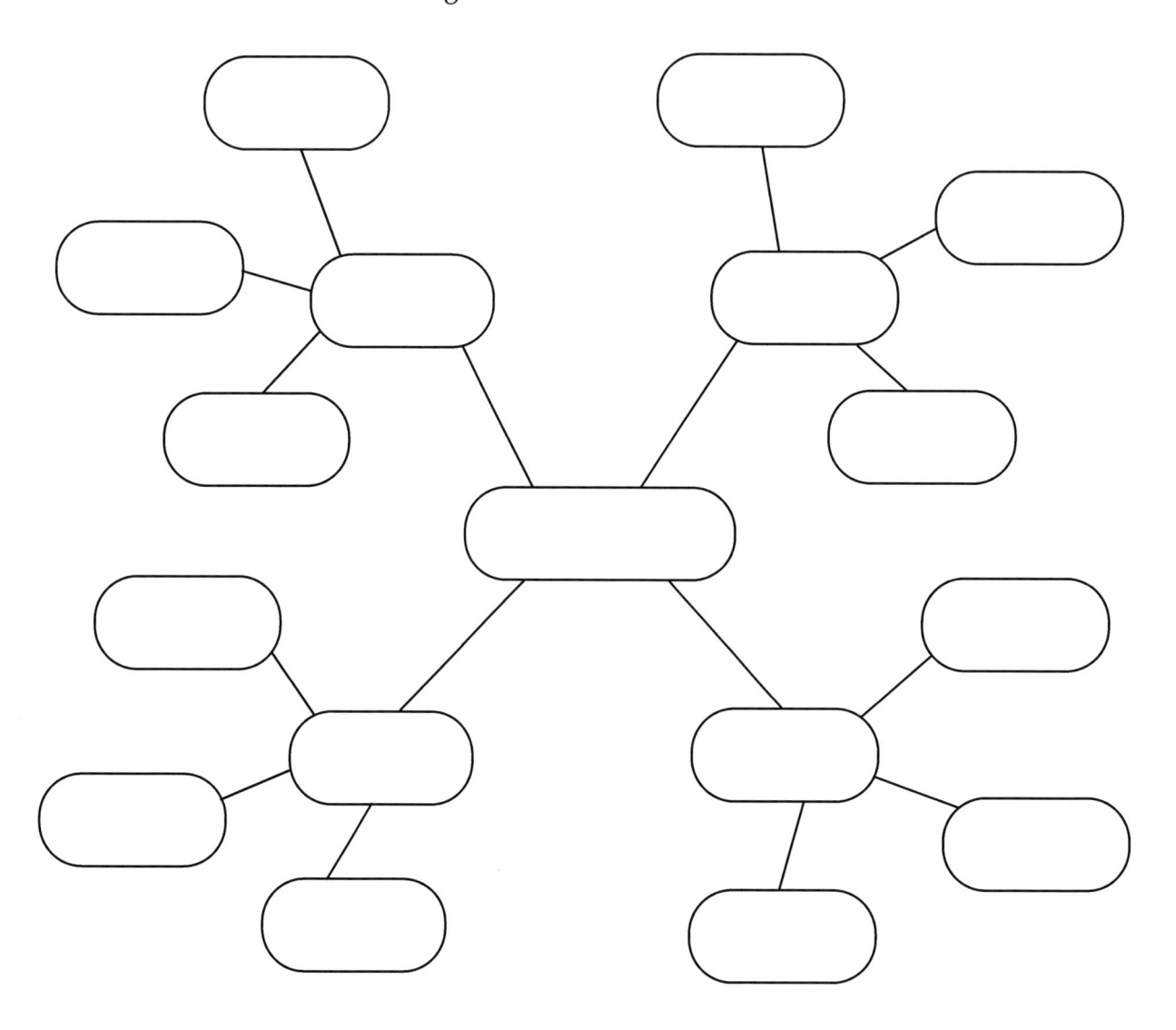

Main Idea and Details Chart

Use this chart to organize your main idea and the details that support it. Add or subtract boxes as needed.

Main Idea

Detail 1

Detail 2

Detail 3

OPINION AND SUPPORTING EVIDENCE CHART

Opinion

Evidence

Evidence

Evidence

Compare and Contrast (Venn) Diagram

Use this diagram to show how two things are similar and different.

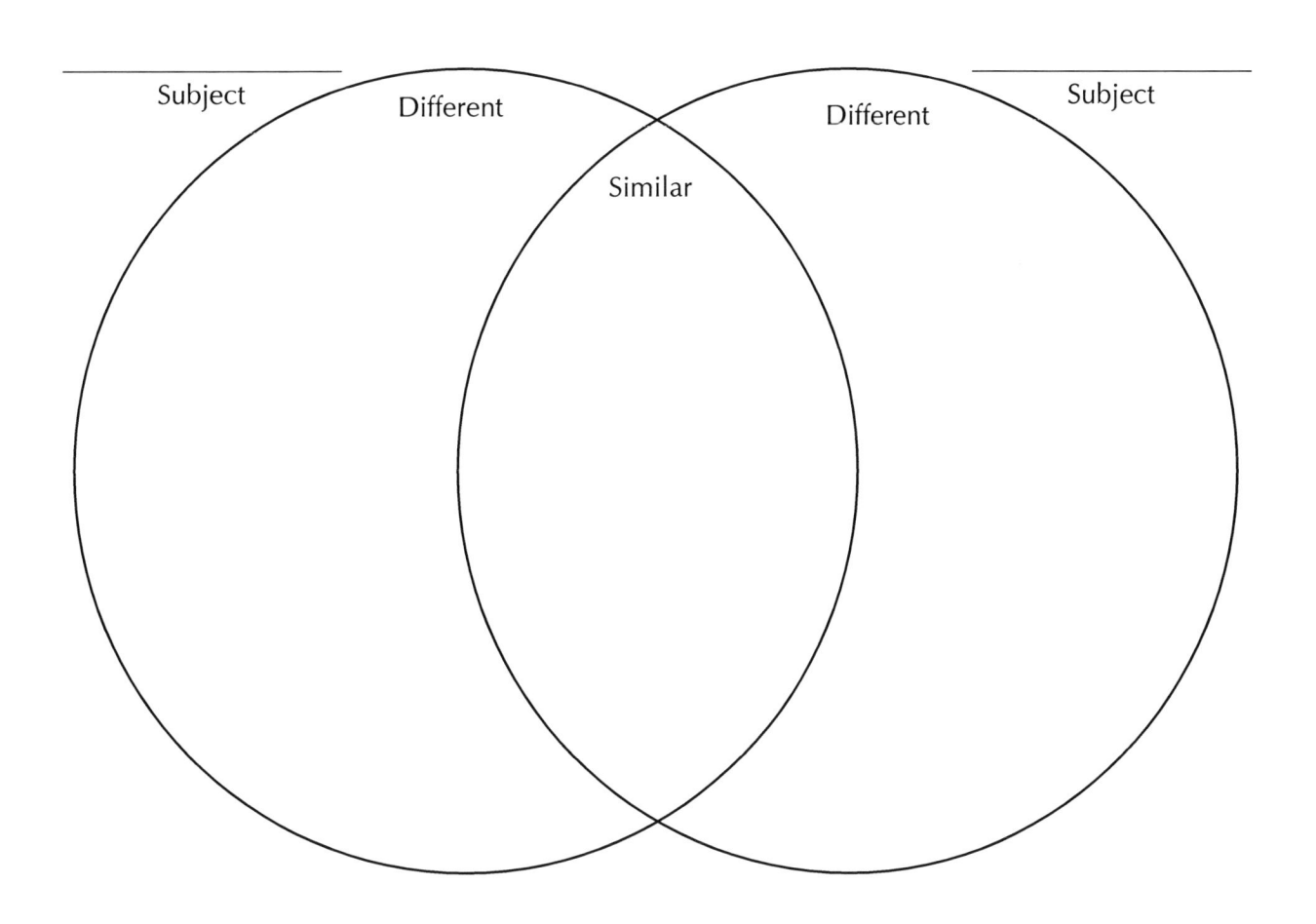

Subject _____   Different   Different   Subject _____

Similar

Cause and Effect Chart

Use this chart to show the relationships between causes and effects. Add or subtract boxes as needed.

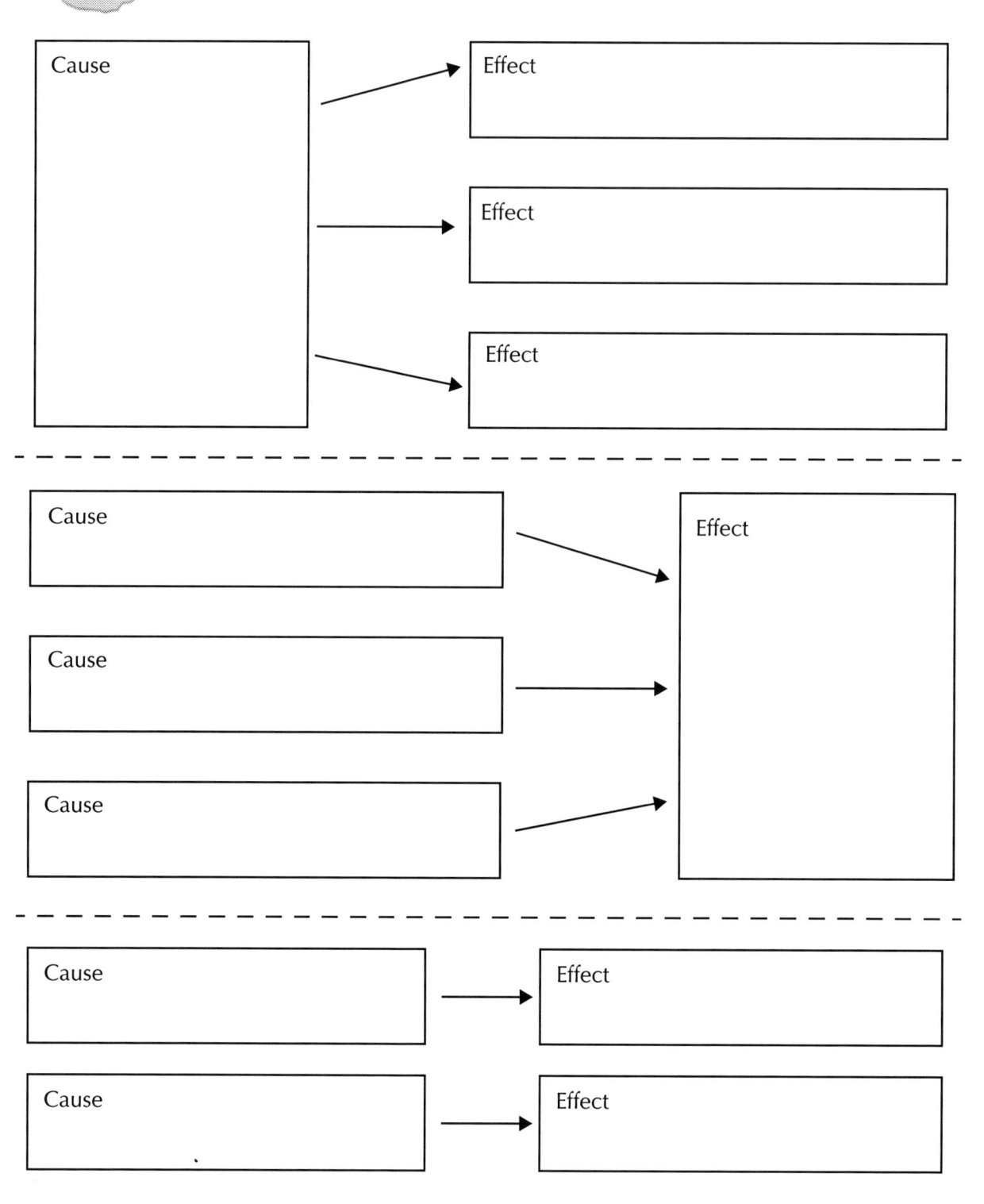

Cause	→	Effect
	→	Effect
	→	Effect

Cause	→	Effect
Cause	→	
Cause	→	

Cause	→	Effect
Cause	→	Effect

CHRONOLOGICAL ORDER CHART

Use this chart to organize events in the order they happened. Add or subtract boxes as needed.

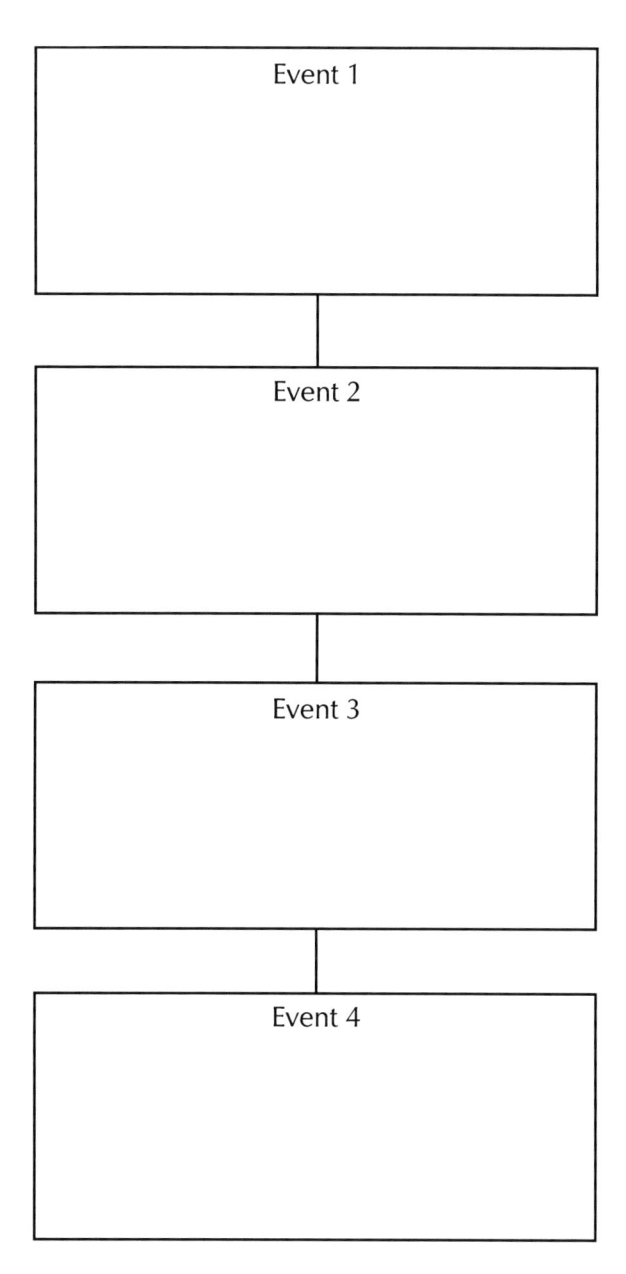

```
┌─────────────────────────┐
│        Event 1          │
│                         │
└─────────────────────────┘
            │
┌─────────────────────────┐
│        Event 2          │
│                         │
└─────────────────────────┘
            │
┌─────────────────────────┐
│        Event 3          │
│                         │
└─────────────────────────┘
            │
┌─────────────────────────┐
│        Event 4          │
│                         │
└─────────────────────────┘
```

REVISING CHECKLIST

The revising step is the time to look back at your writing and handle the big issues, including organization, clarity, completeness, and word choice. Use the checklist below to help you revise your written work. You may want to add some particular problem areas to the bottom of the list.

Organization	Yes	No
Did I use a logical pattern or organization?		
Did I follow my pattern consistently?		
Clarity		
Did I use signal words to clarify my pattern or organization?		
Did I make my purpose clear?		
Did I write a clear thesis statement?		
Did I include any unnecessary sentences?		
Completeness		
Did I include an introduction, a body, and a conclusion?		
Did I include enough information to support my thesis statement?		
Word Choice		
Did I use specific words rather than general words?		
Did I use vocabulary appropriate for my audience?		
Other things to check for:		

Proofreading Checklist

Use the following checklist to polish your written piece before you publish it.

Grammar	Yes	No
Did I write any run-on sentences?		
Did I leave any sentence fragments?		
Do my sentences all make sense?		
Do my subjects and verbs agree?		
Did I use the correct verb tenses?		
Mechanics		
Did I capitalize correctly?		
Did I use commas, periods, semicolons, and colons correctly?		
Did I use apostrophes, question marks, quotation marks, and exclamation points correctly?		
Did I spell everything correctly?		

Peer-Editing Form

Use this form to offer feedback to a classmate—and to receive feedback on your writing.

Some guidelines:

- **Start with praise.** Talk about the best, most interesting, most exciting, most insightful, or most whatever part of the piece.
- **Show respect.** As a writer yourself, you know how hard it can be to put thoughts on paper—you would not want your efforts to be treated lightly.
- **Stick to the point.** Address what you have been asked to address.
- **Be specific.** Saying "This section wasn't clear" is too broad and not very helpful. Something like, "Could you explain more about X? I think I'd understand better how Y happened then" gives the writer a better idea of the problem and a solution.
- **Ask questions.** Revisions are up to the writer. If you phrase your suggestions as questions ("Can you tell more about Z here?" rather than "Tell more about Z"), a writer can respond and then choose to incorporate that change or not.

Writer: _____

Title: _____

Area(s) to be discussed: _____
_____

Good points: _____
_____
_____
_____
_____
_____

Questions: _____
_____
_____
_____
_____
_____

Part 5
Teacher's Guide

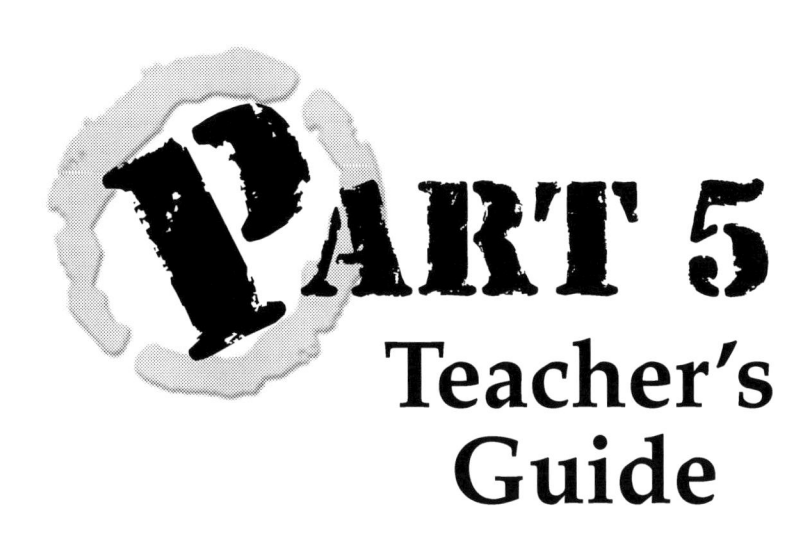

Part 1: Prewriting

Lesson 1: Writing Process Review

This brief lesson reviews the writing process. If students are not yet familiar with the process, this lesson will give them a quick overview. Students who are not familiar with the writing process may need extra modeling.

Lesson 2: Brainstorming

Emphasize that brainstorming is fun—and personal. It is up to the author—the brainstormer—to decide what is and is not worthwhile in a brainstorming session. Students should be encouraged to write whatever comes into their minds, rather than trying to fill out the web neatly or filling in all the circles. In fact, adding or ignoring circles as appropriate shows that students are really letting their ideas flow!

Try It

Webs will vary.

Lesson 3: Narrowing Your Topic

Narrowing a topic need not be a daunting task if students realize that it is greatly to their benefit to do it. This is the time to think about what is most interesting—or, more mercenarily, what is easiest to write about. Having a completed brainstorming web is a great help in choosing a final topic. It helps students "see" what they already know. It can also help them decide what seems most manageable.

Try It

Narrowed topics will vary.

Lesson 4: Purpose

Although students will be tempted to respond "Because I have to" when asked why they are writing an essay, help them move beyond this automatic response and think about what they would like to achieve—besides a decent grade—by writing the particular essay that they will compose. Thinking of a thesis statement as a purpose for writing increases ownership of the piece, and gives students more control. Even if a narrow topic is assigned, students can reword it in a thesis statement of their own.

Try It

Purposes—thesis statements—will vary.

Lesson 5: Audience

The audience for most of students' school essays will be the teacher and, perhaps, classmates. It is important, however, to think about the possibility of other readers; in life, it is not the teacher who will read a memo, a proposal, a letter to the editor, or any other piece of writing. Even in school, it is possible that teachers other than the one who assigned an essay will grade it. And some tests will have complete strangers grading them. Considering one's audience is a sound writing habit to develop.

Good Writing Tip

Answers will vary, but may include some of the following ideas.

1. If the audience were a panel of marine biologists, I would use scientific words and practices without explanation. I could use higher-level vocabulary, and I would assume that the reader knows a lot about the subject.

2. If my audience were a kindergarten class, I would use short words and short sentences. I would try to connect to something they already know, such as pet fish, or sharks they have seen in an aquarium.

3. If this essay were for a newspaper article, I would use vocabulary that I already knew before I read the article—words that pretty much all people my age and older would probably know. I would explain ideas that are not common knowledge, but I wouldn't need to define everything. I would also try to use some hook that would interest the general public in my story.

Part 2: Writing Strategies

This section introduces graphic organizers to help students map out what they will write before they write it. One graphic organizer, the brainstorming web, has already been used. Specific patterns common to language arts are modeled and applied: main idea and details, opinion with supporting evidence, compare and contrast, cause and effect, and chronological order.

Lesson 6: Drafting

The types of daily writing students do will vary, but may include shopping lists, homework lists, notes in class, notes to friends, e-mails, phone messages, appointments, assignment due dates.

The types of writing students do for language arts might include any type of papers; reading, writing, or personal-response journals; and practice writing in various forms, such as friendly letters, business letters, resumes, letters of recommendation, and so on.

Lesson 7: Main Idea and Detail

1. D (that hints at main idea)
2. MI—Stated
3. D
4. D
5. D
6. D
7. D
8. D
9. D
10. D (that hints at main idea)

Transition 1. similarly — Purpose: to show similarities

Transition 2. all in all — Purpose: to conclude

Repeated Idea: Change is the only constant in life; even the best-laid plans are subject to change

Lesson 8: Opinion and Supporting Evidence

1. Passage A
2. probably, I bet, I think
3. March 2001 Massachusetts bill proposal; bill came about as a response to increase in school violence and decrease in standardized test scores; 48% students . . .; 24% students . . .; 35% gang-related
4. Answers will vary.

Lesson 9: Compare and Contrast

1. The compare/contrast words are in stark contrast to, like Haiku, unlike Haiku, while, on the other hand, also, what's more, similarly, more likely than, however.
2. point by point
3. The essay does evaluate each type of pet, giving both the advantages and disadvantages of each. It is intended more to explain, because it does not say that one is better than the other. It explains why one might be preferable in a particular case, but not in general.

Lesson 10: Cause and Effect

1. Main effect: changes in clothing styles
2. Main cause: teenagers' behavior
3. Hip-hop look: baggy jeans, oversized clothing, heel-less and laceless shoes
4. MTV, bands and musicians; CA shoes untied, scrunched-down heels; teens in Soho
5. because, as a result, this observation led to

Lesson 11: Chronological Order

1. Thesis—"Becoming king marked the physical and social decline of Henry VIII"; passage recounts Henry's decline in public eye as his desperation for a male heir takes him through six wives.
2. first wife; wife number two; 1533; 1536 Anne Boleyn was beheaded; days after Anne's execution; this third marriage; shortly after; Henry's fourth marriage; January of 1540; July of that same year; in the latter months of 1540; in 1542; sixth and final wife

Part 3: Practice Readings

This section provides longer selections that students may draw on while writing essays. You may assign the type of essay to be written, or allow students to choose. You may want to suggest the topics listed for each reading, or allow students to generate their own ideas. Any of these readings may be supplemented by student research.

Reading A: Female Athletes and Injury

Possible topics

1. In a well-organized essay, discuss some of the ways female athletes can avoid injuring their ACL.
2. All athletes risk injury when they participate in practice or games. "Female Athletes and Injury" focuses on a particular injury: tearing of the ACL. Do you believe that either Title IX or physiology increases a female athlete's risk of injury?

Reading B: It Can Only Be Love

1. What do you think is the main idea of the article? Support your assertion with evidence from the text.
2. Scientists and researchers have differing opinions about animals' ability to feel emotion. Compare and contrast the arguments of those who do and those who do not believe that animals feel emotion.
3. What evidence exists to support the opinion that animals feel emotion? Support this opinion with evidence from the text, as well as with personal experience, if applicable.

Practice Readings C and D

The following essay topics address these two readings together. Of course, either reading could be used on its own with other topics.

1. The lives of Cisneros and Hernandez shaped their career choices. Compare and contrast the lives of Cisneros and Hernandez, showing how their life experiences affected their career choices. Focus on the experiences the two share and discuss how these experiences shaped their career choices.
2. Trace Cisneros's and Hernandez's lives, from the moment they were born to the present time. Where was Hernandez when Cisneros was born? What were their childhoods and the time they spent in school like? When did the two decide to go to college? What followed their time at college? Did they marry? Find jobs? Provide a chronological breakdown of their lives.

More Topics

The following are some general essay topics that depend on students' own reading and experience. You may assign any of these, as you choose. You may also want to give students a choice of some of these topics.

1. Compare and contrast two of your friends. What makes them similar to one another? What makes them different. Are they more alike than they are different?
2. Focus on a natural phenomenon, like a tsunami, tornado, earthquake, or a rainbow. What causes such phenomena to occur? Explain the causes in detail.
3. Who is your favorite celebrity? Provide a biographical sketch of this person, beginning with her or his birth, and ending with her or his present situation.
4. What is your opinion concerning the death penalty or cloning? Gather evidence in support of your opinion and write a well-organized and fully developed essay that effectively defends your opinion.
5. What do you think is the main idea of Gary Paulsen's *Hatchet*, or Lois Lowry's *The Giver*, or Avi's *Nothing But the Truth*? Support what you choose as the main idea with relevant details from the respective text.
6. Explain how to make a peanut butter and jelly sandwich. Your explanation must be clear enough for someone who has never even heard of a peanut butter and jelly sandwich to follow.
7. What are the effects of global warming, or deforestation, or acid rain? What are the causes of global warming, deforestation, or acid rain?
8. Watch your favorite sports team on television. Provide a play-by-play account of the game. Conclude by telling which team played the better game, and why.
9. Explain why a book you have read should be on a required reading list for schools across the United States.
10. Focus on a character in a book you have read. Discuss the changes this character undergoes over the course of the book.

Part 4: Graphic Organizers

The organizers in this section may be copied for students to use in drafting any writing assignment. The revising and proofreading checklists should be distributed when students are ready to revise and proofread their written work in preparation for publishing them. The peer-editing form, if used, should be distributed during the revision step of the writing process.

Assessment Rubric

The assessment rubric that follows may be customized or modified to suit your needs and those of your students. It may be useful to share the rubric with students before they turn in a written assignment so that they know what to expect in the grading process.

Assessment Rubric

Criteria	1	2	3	4	Score
Organization	Sequence of information is difficult to follow.	Some information poorly placed.	Information presented in reasonable order that reader can follow.	Information presented in logical, interesting order that reader can easily follow.	___
Content Knowledge	Insufficient grasp of information; work does not communicate adequate information.	Writer demonstrates basic understanding of concepts.	Writer is at ease with content.	Writer demonstrates full knowledge of concepts and elaborates.	___
Audience	Writer has not used appropriate tone and/or vocabulary, and has not considered audience's knowledge.	Writer has used some appropriate vocabulary, and has attempted to address audience's knowledge.	Writer has used appropriate tone and vocabulary, and has accurately assessed audience's knowledge.	Writer has used appropriate tone and vocabulary, has accurately assessed audience's knowledge, and has engaged audience with thought-provoking ideas.	___
Completeness	Not enough information; thesis statement not sufficiently supported; no or weak conclusion.	Adequate information; thesis statement supported; weak conclusion.	Sufficient information; thesis statement supported; strong conclusion.	Sufficient information; thesis statement well supported; strong conclusion.	___
Grammar and Mechanics	Piece has four or more grammatical/spelling/usage/punctuation errors.	Piece has three grammatical/spelling/usage/punctuation errors.	Piece has no more than two grammatical/spelling/usage/punctuation errors.	Piece is free of grammatical/spelling/punctuation errors.	___
Other:					___

Comments

Total: ___